Years of HOPE
1921-1929

Alan Skeoch

Grolier Limited
TORONTO

CENTURY OF CANADA SERIES

SERIES CONSULTANT: DESMOND MORTON

Cover Illustrations:

1	2	4
	3	

1. The prime minister, William Lyon Mackenzie King, in London at the Imperial Conference of 1926.
2. Women graduates of the University of Toronto, 1928.
3. A motorist relaxes on the running board of his car in the 1920s.
4. The first contracts issued by the Saskatchewan Wheat Pool, 1924.

I would like to dedicate this book to my wife, Marjorie, whose support and affection has made married life a wonderful experience and who has, in the process, borne Andrew and Kevin, our two sons.

Acknowledgements: Books do not appear by magic. They are the product of much labour by many people whose energies are often overlooked. *Years of Hope* has benefited from the editing of Jocelyn Smyth and Ann Martin. The book has been shepherded through production by Catherine Gordon. It was conceived by Ken Pearson and honed by Desmond Morton. All these people deserve much credit. Above all, however, *Years of Hope* is the result of the life experiences of my mother and father, Elsie and Red, who lived through the years of the twenties with great good humour and optimism.

Illustration credits: Public Archives of Canada, cover (1-C1690) and pages 15 (PA54962), 20 (C9064), 22 (C691), 27 (bottom—C54523), 28 (C21562), 29, 30 (C1690), 36 (C7516), 49 (C16657), 50 (C68509), 66 (C21247), 68 (PA53514), 78 (PA48394), 86, 90 (PA86228); City of Toronto Archives, cover (2) and pages 13, 17 (top left), 34, 95, 103, 106; Private collections, cover (3) and pages 10, 12, 16, 17 (top centre and right, middle right, bottom centre and right), 37, 41 (bottom), 56 (top and bottom), 108; Saskatchewan Archives Board, cover (4) and pages 17 (bottom left), 52, 58-59, 61; Toronto Transit Commission, page 8; Manitoba Archives, pages 17 (middle left: Foote Collection 730), 25 (Hudson's Bay Company Archives), 42 (Foote Collection 119), 44, 71 (courtesy of Ontario Institute for Studies in Education), 82 (Foote Collection 1350), 97 (Foote Collection 289); National Museums of Canada, page 18; Glenbow Alberta Institute, pages 26 (top, courtesy of Ontario Institute for Studies in Education; and bottom), 27 (top, courtesy of Ontario Institute for Studies in Education), 77, 81, 100; Ontario Archives, pages 37, 38, 74, 85, 93, 99; Canadian Pacific Corporate Archives, page 40; City of Vancouver Archives, pages 41 (top), 46; Metropolitan Toronto Library Board, pages 55, 79, 101; Art Gallery of Ontario, page 64 (Bequest of Charles S. Band, 1970); Beeton Institute, College of Cape Breton, page 69; The McMichael Canadian Collection, page 92 (Gift of Mrs. F.B. Housser); Provincial Archives of Alberta, page 105.

Canadian Cataloguing in Publication Data

Skeoch, Alan.
  Years of hope, 1921–1929

(Century of Canada series)
Includes index.   ISBN 0-7172-1860-0

1. Canada - History - 1918–1939.*   2. Canada - Politics and government - 1921–1930.*   3. Canada - Economic conditions - 1918–1945.*   4. Canada - Social conditions - 1918–1930.*   I. Title.   II. Series.

FC570.S54 1987	971.062'2	C87-094465-7
F1034.S54 1987		

CONTENTS

FOREWORD

There was a time when the years between the First World War and the Great Depression were described as "The Roaring Twenties," with a few snatches of Charleston music, a few photos of women in bobbed hair and rolled stockings, and a few references to bathtub gin, gangsters and the bull market on Wall Street.

These images did not apply to Canada nor were they even particularly true about the United States. Very few Canadians played the stock market or could even earn enough to pay income tax. Young people had fun and shocked their elders, just like every generation before and since. The noble experiment of prohibiting liquor had a very different history in Canada and, except for smuggling liquor into the United States, gangsters had little part in it.

More thoughtful historians have called the twenties a decade of dead ends. The Great War inspired Canadians to build a better society. Women had won the vote. Farmers had organized around a radical reform program. Workers had created a strong union movement. Half a million veterans had been involved directly in the struggle for a better world. What was the result? The farm movement fell apart. So did organized labour. A decade after women won the right to vote, a single woman sat in the House of Commons and a single woman was about to be appointed to the Senate. Never had business been more free to prove the glories of free enterprise and the result was the worst economic depression of modern times—after a short dress rehearsal in 1921.

Yet Canadians entered their sixth decade with such brave hopes. And, in a little more time than they had promised themselves, those hopes would be fulfilled. It was in the twenties that Canadians created our first great manufacturing industry. We were, believe it or not, the world's second largest producer of automobiles after the United States. We also began the development of our north, aided by the one truly beneficial technology to grow out of the Great War, the airplane. It was the twenties that saw radio emerge as a truly mass medium, linking Canadians and, even more, North Americans in those shallow images that still shape our memories of the era.

All decades have hopes, despair, achievements and failures and all have something to tell Canadians about themselves, but perhaps the twenties have a special message for an age that is more consious of problems than of solutions. From this distance, we can recognize that the hopeful reformers had more influence than their pessimistic and conservative opponents.

Al Skeoch has been making us aware of our past for a long time, as head of history at Toronto's Parkdale Collegiate Institute, as a historian of our agricultural past on CBC Radio and as a connoisseur and collector of rural artifacts. Built into this book is plenty of evidence of how Al has made history live for his students and a growing audience of radio listeners.

Desmond Morton
Erindale College
University of Toronto

EVENTS 1921–1929

Year	Canada	The World
1921	— Liberals win federal election; Mackenzie King forms first minority government since Confederation. — Agnes Macphail becomes Canada's first woman Member of Parliament. — The Communist Party of Canada is formed.	— Warren G. Harding inaugurated U.S. president. — Hirohito named Prince Regent of Japan. — BBC—British Broadcasting Company (later Corporation)—is formed. — Station KDKA Pittsburgh begins first regular radio broadcasts in U.S.
1922	— Thomas Crerar resigns as leader of the Progressive party. — Women win the vote in Prince Edward Island. — Canada refuses Great Britain's request for military support during the Chanak crisis.	— The U.S.S.R. (Union of Soviet Socialist Republics) is formed. — Mussolini forms Fascist government in Italy. — The Irish Free State is proclaimed. — Turkey becomes a republic.
1923	— The Home Bank collapses. — The Alberta Wheat Pool is established. — Dr. F.G. Banting and Prof. J.J. Macleod are awarded the Nobel Prize for the discovery of insulin. — Foster Hewitt makes the world's first hockey broadcast.	— U.S. state of Oklahoma is placed under martial law because of terrorist activities of the Ku Klux Klan. — Attempted coup by Adolf Hitler fails in Germany. — U.S. President Harding dies; is succeeded by Vice-President Calvin Coolidge.
1924	— Saskatchewan and Manitoba Wheat Pools are formed. — The Royal Canadian Air Force is established. — Regular airmail service in Canada begins.	— Ford Motor Company produces its ten millionth automobile. — Calvin Coolidge wins U.S. presidential election.
1925	— The Conservatives win most seats in the federal election but Liberals remain in office with Progressive support. — Methodists, Presbyterians and Congregationalists join together to form the United Church of Canada.	— First successful television transmission by John Logie Baird. — The Charleston becomes popular. — The Chrysler Corporation is founded. — Adolf Hitler publishes the first volume of *Mein Kampf.*
1926	— Mackenzie King resigns over customs scandal; Arthur Meighen becomes prime minister but is defeated within a few days. — Federal election returns the Liberals. — Vincent Massey becomes the first Canadian ambassador to the U.S.	— Queen Elizabeth II is born. — Hirohito becomes Emperor of Japan. — A.A. Milne publishes *Winnie the Pooh.* — Imperial Conference adopts Arthur Balfour's resolution redefining relationship between Britain and the self-governing dominions.
1927	— Old Age Pension Plan introduced. — Arthur Meighen resigns as Conservative leader and is replaced by R.B. Bennett. — 78 children die in a movie theatre fire in Montreal. — Mazo de la Roche wins the *Atlantic Monthly* prize of $10,000 for her novel *Jalna.*	— *The Jazz Singer,* the first "talking picture," is released. — Charles Lindbergh flies nonstop from New York to Paris in his monoplane, "The Spirit of St. Louis." — The Harlem Globetrotters basketball team is established. — Germany's economic system collapses.
1928	— Percy Williams, Bobbie Rosenfeld and Ethel Catherwood win gold medals in Olympic track and field events. — Morley Callaghan publishes his first novel, *Strange Fugitive.* — *Chatelaine* begins publication.	— Penicillin discovered by Alexander Fleming. — Walt Disney produces the first Mickey Mouse films. — Olympic Games are held in Amsterdam, with women participating for the first time. — Herbert Hoover elected U.S. president.
1929	— Women are officially declared "persons" by the Imperial Privy Council. — Stock market crash on October 29 signals beginning of the Great Depression.	— Museum of Modern Art opens in New York. — Stock markets crash; the Great Depression begins.

PREFACE

It was the backhouse on our family farm that first made me
aware of the twenties. While trying to dodge mosquitoes, I would
distract myself with fantasies inspired by the backhouse walls.
Those walls were papered with old calendars picturing young
women with short dresses, bobbed hair and close-fitting hats,
standing on the running boards of a fascinating variety of automobiles.

At the time, I was far less interested in the girls than in the
cars. They were big, box-like machines, predominantly black,
although the occasional sporty model appeared surrounded by
young men and women holding football or baseball pennants in
their hands. The young men, wearing straw hats with starched
brims, seemed to be challenging the world with their boundless
enthusiasm. The women were equally confident, and some were
even smoking cigarettes and actually driving the Fords, Hupmo-
biles, Dodges and Studebakers along dusty country roads at
breakneck speed.

The backhouse is gone now. In its place, a more antiseptic
but less imaginative structure has been erected. But the memory
of those calendars has endured. So, sadly, have the mosquitoes.

1

LIFE IN THE ROARING TWENTIES:
THE CASE OF ELSIE FREEMAN

Images of the twenties vary. A popular but in many ways inaccurate one is that of widespread prosperity and non-stop good times, of amusement parks, golf courses, baseball games, bootleggers and raised hemlines. These things existed, but they were not part of the lives of all Canadians. It was mostly the middle class that enjoyed them—and it is from the middle class that most writers come. Since they write about what they know, it is their experiences that shaped the popular view of the twenties.

There is another image of the twenties, one to be found in the unglamorous statistics of the decade. Working people lived a tough life, most of them earning less than the $1200 to $1500 a year that was then judged necessary for a family of four to live decently. Only 13 400 Canadian income earners, that is one in 300, were making more than $10,000 per year in 1928.

So, like most periods in human history, the twenties have two faces: one with the grin of success, and the other with the frown of defeat. The frown was by far the more prevalent in 1921. In fact, few people that year would have believed that the label "years of hope" would someday seem appropriate for the decade just begun. Labour unrest across the country had given rise to uneasy feelings about the future. Following the war, soaring inflation persuaded banks to raise interest rates. Although veterans and munition workers found employment in 1919, tight money led to a serious depression in 1921 and thousands of jobs vanished. Nor were international events encouraging. A terrible famine swept Russia. Postwar Europe was a turmoil of unstable new countries, continued fighting and economic chaos.

Despite these and other problems, the twenties became an optimistic decade. Perhaps the end of the war and the halting steps of the new League of Nations helped to fuel this mood. Maybe the economic changes creating a new kind of consumer society helped along these feelings of hope. Whatever the reasons, many Canadians were optimistic once the depression of 1921 lifted.

Like many of her generation, one young Canadian, Elsie Freeman, took hold of the decade with determination and vigour. For her these were indeed *"Years of Hope."* Here is her story.

Mother curled my hair in ringlets as Dad helped pack the cardboard suitcase. Frank was outside hitching up our old horse Bill to the buggy. Before I knew what was happening, the farm was receding behind us as we headed for Acton where I would catch the train for Toronto. It was one of the big turning points in my life.

It was 1918 and I was fifteen years old. Jobs were available for women in Toronto, and I was looking forward to becoming a mother's helper, although I was a little frightened of the big city. Suddenly old Bill

Opposite page:
Bay Street in Toronto, December 1924. By the mid-twenties, electricity and automobiles had transformed Canadian cities, and for the first time the country's urban population outstripped its rural population.

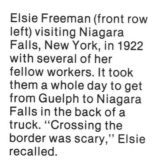
Elsie Freeman (front row left) visiting Niagara Falls, New York, in 1922 with several of her fellow workers. It took them a whole day to get from Guelph to Niagara Falls in the back of a truck. "Crossing the border was scary," Elsie recalled.

staggered and dropped dead in his tracks. Not a good omen. Dad arranged with a nearby farmer to skin Bill and sell the hide to the tannery, and we hiked the rest of the way to town.

The station was busy. Passengers were getting ready. Wagons were loaded with empty milk cans. Freight was piled in heaps down the track. Finally the big steam engine huffed in and ground to a halt, clouds of white steam and black smoke all around. The train seemed to represent what city life was all about: so powerful, so modern, so industrial . . . so frightening. So different from my quiet rural life.

The trip from Acton to Toronto was like a moving picture show, only I was the one moving. We snaked our way through rich farming country, with houses and barns and fields laid out in checkerboard squares marked off with split-rail fences. Then we reached the industrial fringe of Toronto where factory chimneys seemed to greet our coal-fired engine like a long-lost relative.

It was dark when we stopped at Union Station. The high, vaulted ceiling sparkled with electric light bulbs as crowds of strangers moved urgently in all directions. My employer was supposed to meet me. The pink ribbons in my hair would identify me. I waited and waited, but no one came.

In desperation I found a telephone. These

strange machines were still uncommon. I had never used one, so I asked the newsstand girl if she would call for me but she had no time. "It's easy," she said, "just put your nickel in the slot and ask the operator to connect you." I kept putting nickels in but nothing happened. No one mentioned that the telephone had to be lifted off the hook first. Things were not going well.

When I finally connected with my employer, there was no improvement. "I've just come home from downtown," she complained, "and I couldn't possibly come back to meet you." Then she gave me instructions. Streetcars at night? My courage departed, so I got another nickel and phoned my Uncle Chris, who told me to sit and wait till he got there. I bought a newspaper, which turned out to be a scandal sheet called *Hush*, with a lurid picture of a woman on the front. I proceeded to read about a number of strange people and activities associated with the big city. At the same time that Uncle Chris arrived, a large, officious-looking woman approached me.

"Are you Elsie Freeman from Acton?" she demanded, looking at the copy of *Hush* on my knee and at Uncle Chris at my side. Once her first impressions were reversed, the situation improved. The woman had been alerted by Mother just in case something went wrong. She belonged to the Women's Christian Temperance Union, or WCTU. It was a group that protected young people in distress and lobbied government officials to maintain the prohibition of alcoholic beverages.

With the help of both of them, I was soon situated in the house of my new employer. Mrs. M— was not the person I had expected. I felt like a slave, working from dawn to dusk, cleaning and caring for her house and her children. I hated the job. When she asked me to climb out on the third-floor window sill to clean the windows, I decided to quit. One week in Toronto was enough.

I could almost have kissed the cows when I got back home. I even looked forward to getting back to school. Returning home wasn't easy, however, for I felt I was a "quitter." Later I heard that Mrs. M— hired one of the Home Children (young boys and girls sent from Britain to work in Canada), and the girl committed suicide.

My second attempt to join the working class was a little more successful. Dad was finding it tough to earn a living and support his children from our twenty-five-acre (10 ha) farm, and he wanted to buy the farm up the road, which was very hilly but had more arable land. To buy it, we needed more money. During the war, Dad supplemented our family income by working in the Beardmore Munitions Plant in Toronto. In 1918, that job ended. So in 1920, I dragged out the old cardboard suitcase and headed for Toronto once more. Now I was seventeen and a little better prepared for city life.

In Toronto I roomed with Uncle Chris and his new wife, Kitty. I slept on the couch in the kitchen of their two-room house. Working-class people were jammed together in tiny houses and large tenements in the core of the city. The rich lived in mansions in the suburbs, following the example of Sir Henry Pellatt who had built a real castle, Casa Loma. Toronto was a bustling city in 1920 as the war industries converted back to peacetime production. I had no trouble finding a job. The Toronto Pharmaceutical Company paid me $7.50 a week to pack pills and bottle medicines. I worked Monday to Friday from 8:00 A.M. to 5:00 P.M. and then a half-day on Saturday—a forty-four-hour week at around 17 cents an hour.

I was happy as a lark since the other workers were all young girls like myself. Aunt Kitty worked with me for a while but left for a job at Swift's slaughterhouse where the money was better ($9.50). Slaughterhouse work had no appeal to me. Uncle Chris spent his time walking the streets of Toronto selling light bulbs. Electricity was one of the wonders of the decade. Electric lights lit up the night, extended leisure time and led to all kinds of new machines like elevators and electric streetcars. He hoped to cash in on this new technology. But street hawking was tough and he didn't earn as much as Kitty.

I paid them $3.50 for room and board. Streetcar fare cost me about a dollar a week (five tickets for 25 cents), which left me $3.00 a week to buy clothes, entertain myself and send a little back to the farm. All in all, I was pleased. I was optimistic about a promotion when the boss called me to his office one day. But not for long. He showed me a complaint about one of my orders. I had forgotten to empty the sawdust out of a liver pills box, and the box only contained one pill rather than twelve. That sure deflated me. He transferred me to the bottling rooms, a wet, messy place to work. The joy was gone.

Dad wrote me about this time asking if I could come back to help on the farm. So I returned to Acton. And, once again, I returned to school. Woodside School was a one-room schoolhouse located on the hill above our farm. It only had seven pupils in 1920, not enough to keep the school open, so the teacher,

850866

Canadian National Electric Rys
Toronto Suburban District
NO STOP-OVER ALLOWED

Jan.	Feb.	TO	STOP NO.	FROM
Mar.	Apr			**W. TORONTO**
May	Jun	★	1	LAMBTON JUNCTION
July	Aug		12	ISLINGTON
Sept.	Oct	★	18	EATON FARM
Nov.	Dec	★	20	SUMMERVILLE
1	2	★	25	DIXIE
		★	31	COOKSVILLE
3	4	★	33	CENTRE ROAD
5	6	★	38	WINTERS
7	8	★	42	STREETSVILLE
9	10	★	47	MEADOWVALE
		★	50	CHURCHVILLE
11	12	★	52	TOWN LINE
13	14	★	54	HUTTONVILLE
15	16	★	60	NORVAL
17	18	★	70	GEORGETOWN
19	20	★	77	LIMEHOUSE
21	22	★	80	DOLLY VARDEN
23	24	★	85	ACTON
25	26	★	90	BLUE SPRINGS
27	28	★	92	ROCKWOOD ROAD
29	30	★	95	EDEN MILLS
31		★	98	ERAMOSA
		★	99	SPEEDWELL
		★	101	**GUELPH**

EXPRESS	85	90	95	$1
★	65	70	75	80
	45	50	55	60
HALF FARE	25	30	35	40
★	5	10	15	20

PASSENGER'S COUPON   F. C

A ticket for the "radial," an electric railway running between West Toronto and Guelph. Elsie Freeman took this train when she moved to Guelph in 1921.

Miss Major, persuaded my girlfriend Blanche and me to take a bookkeeping course by correspondence. Miss Major took the course as well. It was a pleasant year as the three of us struggled to solve the mysteries of economics while tutoring the seven out-of-school students who ranged from kindergarten age to grade eight.

Late in 1920 an advertisement appeared in the *Acton Free Press:*

HELP WANTED

Fifty girls wanted to learn how to operate electric sewing machines at COLONIAL WHITE WEAR COMPANY, Guelph, Ontario.

Blanche and I were hired and moved to Guelph as the winter of 1921 began. This trip to Guelph was different from my trip to Toronto in 1918. A neighbour drove us to Acton in his automobile, a brand-new Model T Ford. In Acton, we boarded the "radial," an all-electric railway that took us to Guelph in no time at all. It seemed that all these new machines were designed to draw farmers' sons and daughters from the farms to the big cities. Some farmers were even complaining about depopulation of the countryside.

These thirteen women made up the entire female contingent of the class of 1928 at the University of Toronto. Women were beginning to pursue university education in greater numbers than before and one of these graduates, Elsie Gregory MacGill, was the first woman to take a degree in electrical and aeronautical engineering.

Our salary was $9.00 a week until we learned how to run the electric sewing machines. Then we were paid $10.00—nearly 23 cents an hour. We started off making black sateen shirtwaist blouses for the T. Eaton Company. Business was good. From 1921 to 1924, we made these blouses. I was almost eighteen when I started and twenty-one when the job ended.

These were wonderful years. We went to dances two or three times a week, skating parties in the winter, occasional snowshoe hikes and moving picture shows. Dressed in coonskin coats, the boys at the Ontario Agricultural College used to take us to football games; some even came in cars. Like many other young people, I thought this kind of life would go on forever.

But it ended in 1924. Styles changed and soon we were out of work. There was no unemployment insurance in those days and when orders fell off, employees were let go. I lived on my savings until they ran out. Some of my girlfriends went back to the farms. But most of us decided to go to Toronto where skilled sewing machine operators had more chances of finding work.

Almost immediately, I was hired by the T. Eaton Company to make dresses for their catalogue sales department. Many Canadians ordered their clothes through advertisements in the Eaton's catalogue. The work was good. The factory was clean and there was even a nurse available if employees got sick or injured. But the money wasn't as good as it was at the Spadina Avenue dress factories.

The Billy Burke Dress Company approached me to work for them as a sample maker in 1925. A promotion of sorts. There was much more pressure, however, and the working conditions were poor. Cuttings were not swept up steadily and the floors were strewn with pieces of cloth, paper, thread and other garbage. We didn't have a nurse or a doctor to patch us up when the needles cut our fingers, but we were being paid well for the time, around $12.50 a week—nearly 30 cents an hour.

When work slackened, lay-offs occurred. But there were always other companies. Most of them were sweatshops. I never saw any sign of a garment workers union, but if we had known about one, I'm sure we would all have joined. I remember working in one sweatshop on Wellington Street in the basement of a factory. It was unswept and full of mice. We were ordered not to talk or stop work for any reason. It was an inhuman rule, so a friend and I decided to take a break and go to the washroom just to test it. Sharp at

Opposite page:
The wildly popular and highly energetic Charleston got all the publicity, but it did not totally do in older and more sedate dances. These young people are accepting their trophy as the 1929 winners of the annual Waltzing Competition held at Hanlan's Point on the Toronto Islands.

ten o'clock we left our machines and went to the washroom. All the heads in the room stared at us in amazement. From that point on we were closely watched by the foreman.

There was one young girl working for $8.00 a week. She was much younger than the rest of us but a good operator. We told her the rate was $12.50 and to see the Labour Board at the Ontario Parliament Buildings. Shortly afterward, Joyce and I were laid off—a polite way of saying we were fired.

Another place that I worked in 1926 or 1927 was a stuffy little room on College Street. It was jammed with sewing machines. European immigrants were in great demand if they could sew, but not because they worked better than English-speaking girls. The demand was prompted by the fact that they could be paid less. I remember one family in particular. I think they were from Latvia. Both the husband and the wife were hired, and they worked from seven in the morning until late at night. They were anxious to save money to pay the Canadian government for their boat fare from Europe. They bought no furniture and used orange crates for seats until the debt was repaid. They were working hard but they were being cheated. Employers were supposed to give employees 2 percent of their annual wages for holiday pay. The Latvian family didn't know this and got nothing. When I informed them, the boss fired me. So there I was, having to change jobs again. It wouldn't be the last time.

...ges of the twenties.

A working class street in Montreal near the end of the twenties. While a few people cashed in on the prosperity of the roaring twenties, many more lived lives of hardship and deprivation in the cities where they had hoped to make their fortunes.

Some writers have labelled the decade between 1920 and 1929 the "Roaring Twenties." Canadians like Elsie Freeman participated in many of the remarkable changes of those years. She was part of the great movement of Canadians from farms to cities. The growing use of the automobile, the telephone, the radio and electricity was part of this trend. Of course, the wages that gave Elsie a happy life and a few luxuries would have meant poverty for a married person supporting a family. A comfortable family in the twenties, as now, often depended on two or more incomes to support both children and elderly family members.

Elsie was one of a growing group of liberated women who were prepared to find work for themselves. She was quite proud of her ability to use industrial sewing machines, powered by electric motors. She was adaptable and ready to switch jobs when times were slack or when a better job cropped up. Elsie was poor but not depressed; if anything she greeted the twenties with great good humour. She bobbed her hair, an action which shocked her elders and made her something of a rebel. Her experiences were shared by many young Canadians. The twenties were an exciting time to be alive.

REVIEW AND DISCUSSION

Key People and Ideas
Explain the importance of each of the following as they are discussed in the chapter.

Jobs for women   Electricity
Women's Christian Temperance Union   The "radial"
Home Children   The T. Eaton Company

Analysing the Issues
Answer each of the following questions, which deal with important issues raised in the chapter.

1. What were the advantages and disadvantages of city life as opposed to rural life in the 1920s?
2. "Jobs were available for women in Toronto." Why does Elsie Freeman make this statement?
3. Why was immigrant labour in such great demand in the garment shops?

Questions for Discussion
Think carefully about each of the following questions and discuss the issues which they raise.

1. The 1920s brought changes to the lives of many Canadians. Decide whether you think these changes were a good or bad thing, and why. How has life in the twenties affected the life we have today?
2. Do you think our values and attitudes have changed much in the course of the last sixty or seventy years? Give reasons and examples in your answer.

2

CANADA UNDER
MACKENZIE KING

The 1920s brought dramatic changes not only to the lives of ordinary Canadians like Elsie Freeman, but as well to the country's basic institutions and its political leadership. The 1920s marked the beginning of the longest (and perhaps strangest) prime ministerial career in Canadian history.

William Lyon Mackenzie King

King first became prime minister in 1921. He was an introverted man who spent much of his time in office in a lonely, aloof vigil. He was a rambling, boring speaker. Yet Canadians re-elected him time and time again. Why? Because he represented the middle ground. He refused to commit himself either to French-Canadian nationalism or English-Canadian colonialism. He was capable of condemning conscription to French-Canadian Liberals in Quebec in one speech, while flattering western Canadians for their loyalty to the Crown during the First World War in another speech. He supported both labour and management, both east and west, both feminists and male chauvinists, both rugged individualists and moderate socialists. He bound together a diverse nation of immense physical size. The key to his success was his ability to tell people what they wanted to hear.

Who was this man? As a child he was dominated by his mother, Isabel Grace, the daughter of a fiery, partisan man of action, William Lyon Mackenzie, who had been the spark plug of the 1837 Upper Canada Rebellion. King's mother spent much of her time raising her first-born son to be a great man. Through him, she wished to vindicate her father, and she instilled in him a hatred for the Conservatives not unlike the hatred of her father for the old Family Compact.

As King grew up, Canada was fast becoming part of the new, industrial twentieth century. Wages, collective bargaining, strikes and the role of government in labour were emerging as issues in Canadian society. At age seventeen, King entered the University of Toronto. Later, at the University of Chicago and at Harvard, he specialized in economics, taking particular interest in labour and in social reform.

In 1897, King caught the eye of Liberal politicians by exposing the terrible conditions in which workers manufactured uniforms for the militia and the post office. He made sure that the new Laurier government looked good. In 1900, King became Deputy Minister of Labour and soon acquired a reputation for his skill in settling labour disputes. At Sir Wilfrid Laurier's invitation, King entered politics. He was elected to the House of Commons in 1908, and a year later he was appointed Minister of Labour in the Laurier government.

When Laurier's government was defeated in 1911, King lost his seat in the Commons. He worked for the Liberal party in

Opposite page: Mackenzie King campaigning at Cobourg, Ontario, during the 1926 election. King was the dominant politician in Canada through the 1920s and for almost two decades afterwards.

Ottawa and then as a labour relations expert for the Rockefeller Foundation in the United States. He ran in the 1917 election as one of the few prominent English-Canadian politicians to support Laurier's anti-conscription stand and was defeated.

King's loyalty to Sir Wilfrid Laurier and the Liberal party served him well two years later when he ran for the leadership of the party. Liberals chose King as their new leader not because they loved him, but because he was an expert on "modern" issues such as labour and industry and because he stood in the middle on every issue dividing Canadian public opinion. As the *Canadian Forum* stated in 1921, "the man who can restore and foster a spirit of unity between city and country, between Ontario and Quebec on the one hand and Ontario and the West on the other hand, is the man of destiny." King, who took no clear stand on any issue in the election of 1921, appeared to be the man of destiny.

Arthur Meighen: A Contrast in Style

Facing King in the 1921 election was Arthur Meighen. Meighen had taken over as prime minister and leader of the Conservative party when Sir Robert Borden, his health broken by the war, resigned in 1920. A lawyer from Portage La Prairie, Manitoba, Meighen had been one of Borden's most influential and effective ministers. He was a bold, brilliant debater but he had one major electoral disadvantage: in 1917, he had been one of the loudest supporters of conscription, a stand which alienated him from most French-Canadian voters. With courage, Meighen had visited Quebec during the 1921 election campaign. "I never try to ride two horses. I favoured conscription. I introduced the Military Service Act. I spoke for it time and again in the House of Commons, and in every province in the Dominion. I did because I thought it was right." There was something noble in Meighen's actions, but politically his courage was unwise. His debating skill and integrity brought him few friends or converts.

Mackenzie King was a joke in Meighen's eyes. "His words are just the circular pomposity of a man who won't say what he means." In Meighen's view, leadership demanded decisions. It should not be too restricted by the wishes of the people. Canada was such a diverse collection of people and interests that there could be no clear Canadian opinion on any matter. Therefore, Meighen believed, a leader had to make up his own mind. "In our Dominion where sections abound, a Dominion of races, of classes and of creeds, of many languages and many origins, there are times when no Prime Minister can be true to his trust to the nation he has sworn to serve, save at the temporary sacrifice of the party he is appointed to lead."

For Mackenzie King, the heterogeneous nature of Canada

A brilliant parliamentary strategist and debater, Arthur Meighen led the Conservative party from 1920 to 1927. Despite his abilities, Meighen never managed to win broad support from the Canadian electorate, and his political aspirations fell victim to Mackenzie King's shrewd manoeuvering.

was good reason for evading decisions. King liked to spread around the responsibility for decisions and to delay making them as long as possible. Parliament would decide, not he alone. Of course Parliament could only decide issues put before it. If no bills were presented to Parliament, Parliament could make no decisions.

King in Power

The 1921 election results fell just short of producing a Liberal majority. With 116 seats, the Liberals formed the first minority government at the federal level since Confederation. The brand-new Progressive party, with 65 seats, could have formed the official opposition but chose not to, so that role fell to the 50 Conservatives.

The Progressives were the voice of discontented Ontario and prairie farmers. They promised to support the party that favoured their interests. However, those interests were diverse. Many Manitoba and Saskatchewan Progressives, including party leader Thomas Crerar, wanted low tariffs, a return to grass-roots rural democracy, and a reduction in the power and influence of the protectionist forces centred in Ontario. Most importantly, they wanted "a Western Voice." Most Ontario and Alberta Progressives, on the other hand, wanted a total reorganization of the political system. They were greatly influenced by Henry Wise Wood's theory of group government. Wood and his followers wanted to do away with political parties in favour of government in which groups such as farmers, merchants and labour would be represented. Despite the Progressives' considerable numbers in Parliament, this fundamental disagreement within the party weakened it.

Mackenzie King saw an opportunity to use his skills as a mediator to draw the Progressives into the Liberal fold and soon had an agreement of support from them. It was only a matter of time, he hoped, before the Progressives became Liberals.

One issue which soon put King's accommodation with the Progressives to the test was that of railway freight rates. Freight rates were a sacred cause for western farmers. Wheat prices had plummeted from $2.38 a bushel in 1919 to $1.11 a bushel in 1921. Farmers were in acute distress, and many would soon have to face the choice of farming at the poverty level or selling out and moving to the expanding cities.

The issue of freight rates went back more than a quarter of a century. Almost from the day the prairies produced their first crops, western farmers had complained about the rates the Canadian Pacific Railway charged to ship their grain to eastern markets. Then, in 1897, the CPR needed financial help to build the railway line through the Crow's Nest Pass in British Columbia

Tariffs
*The tariff issue was not
new. From Macdonald's
days prime ministers had
been besieged by western
farmers clamouring for an
end to tariffs. In 1910 Sir
Wilfrid Laurier had
listened to them and run for
re-election on a platform
that included a free trade
agreement with the United
States. The reasons for his
ensuing defeat were
complex, but not least
among them was a high-
powered propaganda
campaign mounted by
eastern business interests
that convinced droves of
workers that their jobs
were in jeopardy.*

and appealed for a federal government subsidy. In return for this subsidy, the government asked for a reduction in freight rates on grain and flour heading east and manufactured goods moving west. The Crow's Nest Pass Agreement, 1897, made these reduced rates statutory. In 1919, these rates were suspended for three years for reconsideration. In 1922, a decision had to be made. Should the CPR be forced to continue giving special rate concessions to western farmers? Advised by Sir Clifford Sifton, Laurier's one-time senior minister from the West, Mackenzie King decided to partially restore the old rates.

Throughout the early twenties, Mackenzie King and the Liberals continued to court the Progressives. Both parties supported tariff reform, although the Progressives would have preferred more radical action than the Liberals. With this common issue, the Progressives were reluctant to topple King's minority government. Such a move would bring Meighen and the Conservatives into power and thereby assure high tariffs. Mackenzie King was careful not to offend the Progressives, referring to them as "Liberals in a hurry." Slight tariff reductions were introduced. "I want, if I can, to have the west feel that I am its friend," asserted King. He also knew that the only tariff reforms his Quebec supporters wanted were higher tariffs. A Liberal leader could not easily take a clear stand.

Mackenzie King's blandishments were having the desired effect. Many Progressive supporters and members began to look more favourably on the Liberals. Meanwhile, the split within the Progressive party was becoming more pronounced. Crerar resigned as leader in 1922, and his successor, Robert Forke, was unable to heal the division. Rising wheat prices in the mid-twenties dispelled much of the prairie discontent that had expressed itself in Progressive votes. More and more Progressives were ready to shift their support.

The Elections of 1925 and 1926

The shift in Progressive support was reflected in the results of the election in 1925. The Progressives dropped to 24 seats. This was small consolation to Mackenzie King and the Liberals. Their strength dropped from 116 seats to 99, as Ontario and the Maritimes turned to the Conservatives. Meighen's party won 116 seats, the largest number, but not a majority. As was his right, Mackenzie King decided not to resign, counting on the support of the Progressive fragment to give him a majority in the House.

So began one of the most peculiar years in Canadian parliamentary history. The party with the most seats was not asked to form a government. Instead, the party that had come second tried to govern. It might have worked; corruption dashed the experiment.

High-level customs officials were caught accepting bribes and covering up for rum-runners who were smuggling alcohol into the United States. The so-called "Customs Scandal" confirmed the general belief of Progressives that the old parties were corrupt. King knew he could not count on their support as the Conservatives prepared to put forward a motion of no confidence in the House of Commons. Rather than be censured by the House, as he surely would, he asked the Governor General, Lord Byng, for a dissolution of Parliament and a new election. The Governor General refused. He pointed out that Arthur Meighen's Conservatives had more seats than the Liberals and should have a chance to form a government before the country was put to the expense of an election. King immediately resigned, convinced that Byng had given him a constitutional issue by refusing his prime minister's request.

Meighen needed the support of the Progressives if he was to form a government. This support, though given initially, soon wavered, and four days later Meighen's government fell. The ensuing election was waged by the Liberals on the constitutional issue. How dare a British-appointed Governor General interfere with Canadian affairs? In Quebec and across the West, indignation was easily aroused. Yet we know that there were other, deeper issues at work.

Canada was prospering. J.A. Robb, King's finance minister, had introduced large and popular tax cuts. J.W. Dafoe, the influential editor of the Manitoba *Free Press,* had persuaded

Lord Byng, Governor General of Canada from 1921 to 1926, being made an honorary chief of the Cree during a historical pageant given by the city of Edmonton and the Hudson's Bay Company.

WOMEN'S RIGHTS

The campaign for women's rights in Canada made some important advances in the 1920s. The decade began with the 1921 federal election, the first national election to be held since all Canadian women over twenty-one won the right to vote and to stand for public office. The struggle for voting rights for women had been part of a broader reform movement, and some of its more idealistic supporters had hoped for revolutionary changes in politics and society as a result of women voting for the first time. The entry of women into politics, they believed, would safeguard prohibition and ensure other reforms such as an end to child labour and improvements in public health and women's working conditions.

The real results fell short of these dramatic expectations. Women did not vote in a block for reformist candidates and parties. Of the five women who ran for office in the 1921 election, only one, Agnes Macphail, a teacher who ran for the Progressives in a rural Ontario constituency, was elected. She was re-elected four times but remained the only woman in the House of Commons until 1935.

By 1922 when women in Prince Edward Island won the vote, every province except Quebec had acknowledged the right of women to participate in provincial elections. As in federal politics, the number of women elected in the provinces in the twenties was small. The victories were all in the west. Mary Ellen Smith, who had been elected to the British Columbia legislature in 1918, became the first woman cabinet minister in the British Empire in 1921. In Alberta in the same year Irene Parlby of the United Farmers became the second when she was elected to the provincial legislature, along with Nellie McClung, a Liberal. Once in office these women continued the campaign for social reform that had accompanied the suffrage movement.

Women were also entering public life in Canada through channels other than electoral politics. Emily Murphy had become the first woman judge in Canada when she was made a police magistrate in Alberta in 1916. She was soon joined by Alice Jamieson, and in 1917 by Helen Gregory MacGill in British Columbia. It was in this context that women's most important legal advance in the twenties, the Persons Case, developed. Lawyers appearing in court before Murphy and Jamieson argued that women could not be judges because they were not "persons" under the law. In 1917 the Supreme Court of Alberta ruled on the point, declaring that given changing times and attitudes women were unquestionably persons.

This ruling resolved the question in Alberta, but Murphy was concerned about the status of

During her fourteen years in the Alberta cabinet, Irene Parlby fought for the rights of immigrants, farmers and women, and for improved public health services and education.

women elsewhere in the country. To put the issue to the test nationally, she enlisted support at a Federal Women's Institute conference in 1919 for a resolution requesting that the prime minister appoint a woman to the Senate. The National Council of Women backed the move, and in 1921 the Montreal Women's Club took it a step further by asking that Emily Murphy herself be made a senator. The prime minister, Arthur Meighen, turned down the request on the grounds that women were not persons under the British North America Act and therefore were not eligible for Senate appointments.

Murphy later discovered that an obscure

Emily Murphy campaigned for a wide range of reforms affecting women and children. She also wrote extensively under the pen name "Janey Canuck."

section of the Supreme Court Act allowed any five individuals to request an interpretation of the BNA Act from the Supreme Court of Canada. Murphy and four other prominent activists in the women's movement, Nellie McClung, Henrietta Muir Edwards, Irene Parlby and Louise McKinney, submitted their petition to the court in 1927 and the case was heard early in 1928. When the court ruled against them, the women decided to take their case to the Judicial Committee of the Imperial Privy Council in England, which was still Canada's final court of appeal on constitutional matters. They were backed not only by the Alberta government but also by the federal government which, along with Quebec, had opposed them before the Supreme Court of Canada. In 1929 the Privy Council ruled strongly in favour of the women's claim, stating that "the exclusion of women from all public offices is a relic of days more barbarous than ours" and that women were indeed persons and therefore just as eligible as men for Senate appointments.

Again, just as the immediate practical impact of women winning the vote was limited, so too were the consequences of the Persons Case. To many people, the point of law seemed overly obscure and technical. One woman reading the newspaper coverage of the case commented, " 'Privy Council finds women are persons.' Well, aren't they smart —I wonder what they thought we were?" The impact of the judgement was further blunted when Mackenzie King chose Cairine Wilson as the first woman senator in 1930. Wilson was very much a member of the political establishment. Her loyalty was entirely to the Liberal party and not to the struggle for women's rights.

Although she had no formal legal training, Henrietta Muir Edwards became an expert on the laws affecting women and children in Canada.

The practical gains made by women in the 1920s were more limited than many had hoped, but the Persons Case was nonetheless of tremendous symbolic importance. This victory, along with the political gains made at both the provincial and federal levels, laid the basis for further advances in the decades to come.

In 1938 the prime minister, Mackenzie King, unveiled a tablet honouring the women who won the Persons Case. Senator Cairine Wilson (back row, right) and Nellie McClung (front row, right) were among those present for the occasion.

himself that the Tories should not be allowed back to power and he shared his conviction with prairie readers. Mackenzie King was perhaps the lesser of two evils but he had supported lower tariffs on foreign-made farm equipment, he had restored the Crow's Nest Pass freight rate agreement as it applied to wheat and flour. He had supported the prairie dream of an outlet to the ocean by way of a railway to Hudson Bay. A railway and a port would give the west an alternative to the Great Lakes–St. Lawrence route to European markets.

When the votes were counted, Ontario and British Columbia remained loyal to Meighen but the rest of the country returned to King. The Liberals held 128 seats while the Conservatives dropped to 99. Arthur Meighen, defeated in his own riding of Portage La Prairie, resigned as Tory leader in 1927. His successor was Calgary lawyer and heir to the Eddy Match fortune, Richard Bedford Bennett. Quebec could be reminded that Bennett had left Parliament in 1917 rather than support conscription. The Progressives, with only 20 seats, continued their decline. Only a small "Ginger Group" survived with a handful of Albertans and Canada's only woman MP, Agnes Macphail, making common cause with J.S. Woodsworth's tiny Labour group.

For the rest of the decade, Mackenzie King kept his head down, paid off a few debts, and allowed the new buoyancy of the Canadian economy to carry his government's popularity. In 1927, he followed through on his promise to finish the long-awaited Hudson Bay Railway. After bickering over the route and selection of the mouth of the Churchill River as its terminus, the railway was completed in 1929 at a cost of more than $45 million.

In 1925, Woodsworth's tiny Labour party had squeezed a pledge of old-age pensions from King in return for their support. After a Senate veto in 1926, King kept his promise in 1927. Ottawa agreed to pay half of a twenty-dollar monthly pension to needy Canadians over the age of seventy. The other half of the money was to be provided by provincial governments, which would also administer payment. Even with the strict means test that kept down the numbers of those who qualified, several provinces were reluctant to commit themselves to the expenditure. British Columbia was the first to participate, followed soon by Ontario and the three prairie provinces. The Maritime provinces joined in 1931 after the new Conservative prime minister, R.B. Bennett, raised the federal share to 75 percent. Quebec waited until 1936. One interesting side effect of the pension scheme: several provinces that had retained prohibition (Ontario, New Brunswick, Nova Scotia) dropped it so that liquor revenues could help pay the cost of the pensions.

King's low-key government worked smoothly enough as long as Canada remained prosperous. But what happened when

In 1921 Agnes Macphail became Canada's first woman MP. She held her seat for nineteen years and worked for prison reform, pensions, better health services and legislation that would benefit farmers. Commenting on her position as the only woman in the House of Commons, Macphail wrote, "People in the gallery pointed me out and said, 'Right there. That's her!' . . . I couldn't open my mouth to say the simplest thing without it appearing in the papers. I was a curiosity, a freak. And you know the way the world treats freaks."

Winnipeg *Free Press* cartoonist Arch Dale satirizes the alliance Mackenzie King formed with Labour and Progressive MPs at the expense of Arthur Meighen and the Conservatives. King's promise to introduce old-age pensions won him the support of the smaller parties in the Commons.

the economy began to collapse at the end of the decade? Was Ottawa responsible for farm bankruptcies or for unemployment relief? Constitutionally, these were matters of provincial concern. Lawyers and politicians argued that Ottawa had a responsibility to act in an emergency, but it was hard for King and the Liberals to admit, after almost a decade in power, that Canada was in an economic mess.

King made it clear that he would not give financial help to any provincial government that was constantly carping and criticizing him. "No, not a five-cent piece," he told Tory MPs clamouring for help for Ontario. Sympathetic prairie governments were another matter. The "five cents" was all anyone heard. For once in his life, Mackenzie King had tripped on his tongue. All his careful election speeches during the 1930 campaign, and all the distribution of patronage and benefits could not undo the damage. If the Liberals would not act in the economic crisis, R.B. Bennett would.

Elegant in morning coat, striped trousers and spats, Bennett was the model of a successful businessman. His millions financed the Conservative campaign. His booming voice, amplified by the new microphones, gave Canadians confidence that someone was listening to them and that Mr. Bennett really could "blast a way into the markets of the world" by raising tariffs. Farmers might have their doubts but here was a man from their region. Quebeckers, too, knew that Bennett was one Tory who had opposed conscription. Rural voters blamed King for letting New Zealand butter compete with their dairy products. That would not happen under Bennett.

To King's shock and indignation, his party was unexpectedly and badly defeated on July 28th—only 91 Liberals would face

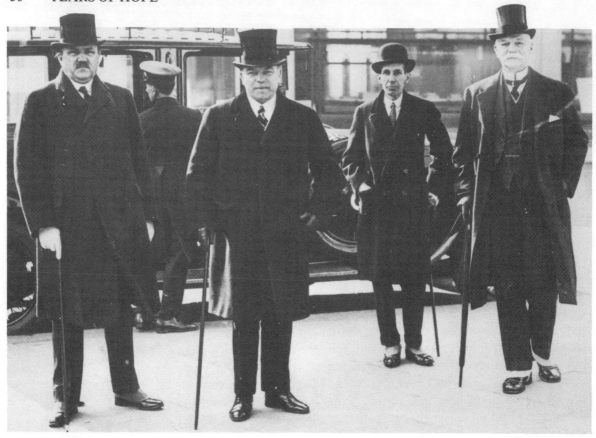

Mackenzie King (second from left) at the Imperial Conference of 1926 in London. With him are (from left to right) Ernest Lapointe, Minister of Justice and King's Quebec lieutenant and most important adviser; Vincent Massey, Canada's first ambassador to the United States; and Peter Larkin, Canada's high commissioner to Britain.

137 Conservatives. The Progressives had dwindled to 12; Woodsworth's group grew to only 3.

International Relations during the 1920s

Despite Canada's insistence on becoming a full-fledged member of the League of Nations when it was established after the First World War, Canadians were settling back into a kind of isolationism by the early 1920s. With its headquarters in Geneva, Switzerland, the League was remote from North American shores. The fact that the United States had refused to join made it seem even more remote from North American concerns. Most Canadians tended to see it as a European-dominated organization, serving mainly European interests, and as such they distrusted it. "We think in terms of peace," said Senator Raoul Dandurand, Canadian delegate to the League Assembly in 1924, "while Europe, an armed camp, thinks in terms of war . . . . We live in a fire-proof house, far from inflammable materials."

Many Canadians also feared that Canada's newly-won independence would be compromised if it became too enthusiastic a member of the League. This point of view had been expressed by Lucien Cannon, a member of Parliament, in 1919: "I am not in favour of England ruling this country, but I would rather be ruled by England than by Geneva." Mackenzie King's own view was not dissimilar. One historian describes King's attitude to the League as one of "studied neglect."

Nor did Mackenzie King want Canada to play a subservient role within the British Empire. The Imperial War Cabinet, established in 1917, had conceded that the Dominions should have some influence over imperial foreign policy. Meetings of member countries of the Empire were continued after the war in imperial conferences. The Dominions would continue to have a say in imperial foreign policy—and they would continue to be expected to support it.

Influence over a common foreign policy was not what King wanted, however. He wanted Canada to be free to establish its own. The opportunity to make his point came in 1922 with the Chanak crisis, named after the small Turkish seaport that was the focus of the controversy. Although Turkey had acknowledged defeat when it signed the Treaty of Sèvres in 1920, the agreement had not been respected. Turkish nationalists drove the Greeks from Smyrna and quarrelled with British occupation troops. By September of 1922 a British occupation force was pinned down at Chanak in the Straits of the Dardanelles. Turkey and Britain seemed on the verge of war.

Britain saw the Chanak crisis as an opportunity to test both the new imperial relationship and the wartime settlement and called upon the other member countries of the Empire to contribute soldiers. King refused to let Canada get involved. "I am sure the people of Canada are against participation in this European war," he wrote in his diary. His public statements were much less direct. "We have not thought it necessary to reassert the loyalty of Canada to the British Empire . . . rest assured that, should it become necessary to summon Parliament, Canada, by decision of its Parliament, will so act as to carry out the full duty of the Canadian people." Nevertheless, these words meant no to the British request.

A hurriedly assembled peace conference, at which Canada did not participate, soon put an end to the crisis. For Canadians, its main significance was the death of a common imperial foreign policy. At an imperial conference the year after the Chanak affair, the right to make separate treaties was formally extended to all Dominions.

That same year marked the first occasion on which Canada signed a treaty on its own behalf with the United States. Previously, all such treaties had been handled directly by Britain. The Halibut Fishing Treaty signed on 2 March 1923, which regulated fishing off the North American coast, began as a formal arrangement between Britain and the United States but ended as an agreement strictly between Canada and the United States. In 1925 King reinforced his emphasis on an independent foreign

League of Nations
The League of Nations was established in 1919 at the Paris Peace Conference to secure and keep peace through arbitration. By the early thirties, the League had lost much of its influence and disintegrated entirely during the Second World War. Its successor, the United Nations Organization, was formed in 1945 after the war ended. Canada was a member of the League throughout its existence and a founding member of the United Nations.

policy for Canada by appointing O.D. Skelton undersecretary of state for external affairs. Until his death in 1941, Skelton played a key role in directing Canada's foreign policy and developing its civil service.

The change in the status of the Dominions implicit in the decision of the 1923 Imperial Conference was acknowledged at the next conference in 1926 in what is known as the Balfour Declaration. Named after its author, Arthur Balfour, a former prime minister of Great Britain, this document declared that Britain and the Dominions of Canada, Australia, New Zealand, South Africa, Newfoundland and the Irish Free State were "autonomous communities within the British Empire, equal in status, in no way subordinate one to another in any aspect of their domestic or external affairs, though united by a common allegiance to the Crown, and freely associated as members of the British Commonwealth of Nations."

With the exception of two significant areas, real independence had been achieved and would be formally confirmed by the Statute of Westminster in 1931. The exceptions were not Britain's doing. Federal and provincial governments had to agree on a formula for amending Canada's constitution, the British North America Act, before it could pass into Canadian control. Thanks largely to the resistance of Ontario's Tory premier, Howard Ferguson, and his Quebec Liberal counterpart, Louis-Alexandre Taschereau, the provinces and Ottawa failed to agree on a formula. The power to amend the BNA Act thus remained, at Canada's request, in British hands—where it would stay for another fifty years. For similar reasons, the Judicial Committee of the British Privy Council remained the final court of appeal for Canadian constitutional cases until 1947.

Not all Canadians were enthusiastic about the apparent weakening of the close relationship between Britain and Canada. Some worried that independence from Britain would mean stronger links with the United States—perhaps even political union. They considered the British connection essential to the maintenance of a distinct Canadian identity, able to resist the overwhelming influence of the United States.

In 1926, Vincent Massey was appointed the first Canadian ambassador to the United States. One disgruntled Canadian wrote: "I hereby give you warning that if you are appointed to the position I will personally finish your course with a knife in your belly; shooting is too good for you, and I'm not afraid of hanging for principle." Nothing happened, but as Massey commented, "the letter did reflect a popular attitude towards the establishment of the post."

Two years later, a Canadian mission opened in Paris, and another in Tokyo the following year.

REVIEW AND DISCUSSION

Key People and Ideas
Explain the importance of each of the following as they are discussed in the chapter.

William Lyon Mackenzie King
Arthur Meighen
Lord Byng
Agnes Macphail
J.S. Woodsworth
Vincent Massey

The Progressives
The Customs Scandal
Old-age pensions
League of Nations
Balfour Declaration

Analysing the Issues
Answer each of the following questions, which deal with important issues raised in the chapter.

1. What were the main political issues to emerge in the early twenties? Why?
2. Why was Mackenzie King considered to be a "man of destiny"?
3. How did the political beliefs and philosophies of King and Meighen differ?
4. What factors led to the King–Byng dispute?
5. Why was Canada's membership in the League of Nations generally unpopular in the country?

Questions for Discussion
Think carefully about each of the following questions and discuss the issues which they raise.

1. Mackenzie King represented the middle ground in most political issues. Would it be true to say he was a weak leader because of this? Be prepared to back up your answer with facts.
2. The establishment of old-age pensions was the most important contribution Mackenzie King made to Canada's development. Do you agree or disagree? Why?

3

PROVINCIAL POLITICS

Many of the issues which dominated federal politics in the 1920s had consequences at the provincial level as well. These years were relatively uneventful in some parts of the country, but in a number of the provinces there were important developments, particularly in the first half of the decade.

Ontario

Just as the Progressive party was an important factor in federal politics in the early 1920s, so too were farm movements and parties in several of the provinces. The issues which motivated these groups differed widely from one province or region to another. And even within individual provincial parties, there was often dissension and disagreement, just as there was in the federal Progressive party.

Farm leaders had real economic goals. They wanted to improve the prices farmers got for their products and to cut the costs of farming and rural life. They wanted better roads—but not so good that city people would invade the countryside or that their own sons and daughters would go down those roads to the city. But rural leaders believed that they were also protecting a superior way of life. Because farmers were "primary producers," actually creating value from their fields and livestock, they considered themselves to be morally superior to people who merely manipulated money, such as bankers and stockbrokers. Farm life demanded long hours and rural people had little sympathy with workers who wanted an eight-hour day.

The farm protest movement achieved its first provincial victory in Ontario. In October 1919 the United Farmers of Ontario (UFO) won a stunning victory over the Conservatives, who had formed the previous government. With the support of Labour and independent members, the UFO had a slim majority over the combined forces of the Liberals and Conservatives.

One of the key issues which drew support to the UFO was rural depopulation. Canada was in the process of transforming itself from a rural to an urban society. The 1921 census would reveal that by a very narrow margin more Canadians lived in the city than in the country. The trend towards urbanization was more advanced in Ontario (58 percent) than in most of the other provinces. This shift was already evident in 1919, but the rural population still controlled a majority of the seats in the provincial legislature. The United Farmers and their supporters wanted to make the most of their power while they still had it. Their appeal to voters was based on their defence of the rural way of life and the values they associated with it.

The UFO's victory was so unexpected that they did not manage to choose their leader, Ernest C. Drury, a Simcoe County farmer, until a month after the election; he did not win a seat in

Opposite page: Road construction near Oakville, Ontario, in the early twenties. Cars needed good roads, and concrete surfaces began to replace the dirt roads that linked most of the big cities. The boom in road construction was just one of the spin-offs of the automobile revolution.

the legislature until a by-election was held in Elsie Freeman's home county of Halton in 1920.

Lack of organization continued to characterize the UFO government. The party was badly split between those who saw their electoral victory as an opportunity to bring in radical farmers' reforms and those who, like Drury himself, were in favour of "broadening out"—providing broad-based, stable and efficient government for the province as a whole.

The differing attitudes toward road construction were typical of the disunity within the UFO. The more radical members wanted rural roads improved but not highways, which they regarded as a threat to the rural way of life because they facilitated travel from the country to the city. Drury and his more moderate colleagues were committed to improving both highways and secondary roads across the province, and their view won in the end—but at considerable cost to party unity.

One of the chief representatives of the radical farmers was the party secretary, J.J. Morrison. A strong supporter of Wood's theory of group government, Morrison insisted that the UFO should serve only the interests of farmers and reject any conventional form of party loyalty and organization. As far as Morrison was concerned, the *only* issue in Ontario was rural depopulation. His position brought him repeatedly and openly into conflict with Drury and the moderates, and this was a significant factor in the collapse of the UFO.

Despite their internal difficulties, the UFO did introduce sound policies in a number of areas. In addition to their expansion of the province's highways and roads, they made improvements in civil service pensions, university funding, rural education and hydro-electric services. They were less successful in other areas. The zealous enforcement of prohibition by the attorney general, W.E. Raney, alienated voters, particularly in the new urban centres. The UFO failure to give any solid support to Regulation 17, which limited the teaching of French in Ontario schools, alienated the more extreme Protestant voters. Finally, the United Farmers withdrew their support from the Drury government because it had looked beyond the interests of the rural community in shaping its policies. By the 1923 election, the combination of party disunity and alienated voters doomed the UFO government. Drury himself grew weary and short-tempered. He called a snap election after members of the UFO had been found drinking bootleg liquor in the Legislature during an all-night session. The Conservatives led by Howard Ferguson won by a landslide.

The new Conservative government was well organized under Ferguson's strong leadership. He was a shrewd politician whose adroit management of the province's affairs earned him the nickname "Foxie Fergie." The gradual withdrawal of prohibition

Sir Frederick Banting, co-discoverer of insulin, which is used in the treatment of diabetes. Along with one of his colleagues, J.J.R. Macleod, Banting was awarded the Nobel Prize for medicine in 1923.

between 1924 and 1927 was typical of Ferguson's smooth methods. Recognizing that a tax on the sale of alcohol would greatly increase the province's revenues, Ferguson was determined to end prohibition. He set about it gradually, equally determined not to suffer any political damage in the process. In a 1924 referendum, 51.5 percent of Ontarians voted in favour of retaining prohibition. To placate the 48.5 percent who voted against it, in 1925 the government permitted the sale of beer with 4.4 percent alcohol content, on the grounds that it was too weak to be intoxicating. This beer became popularly known as "Fergie's Foam." With these preparatory steps taken, Ferguson felt able to campaign in the 1926 election for government control of the sale of alcohol. He won easily. By 1927 prohibition was dead, and the Ontario treasury began to profit enormously from the sale of alcohol.

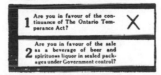
An advertisement supporting the prohibition cause in the 1924 Ontario referendum.

Four prominent figures in business and politics at the end of the twenties. From left to right, Sir Edward Beatty of the CPR, Lord Willingdon, the Governor General, R.B. Bennett, the leader of the Conservative party, and Howard Ferguson, Conservative premier of Ontario.

Ferguson's government was active in other areas as well. More roads, hospitals and schools were built. The development of the province's natural resources, especially in the north, was encouraged. Ferguson was particularly concerned with hydroelectric development. He was determined that the province should have jurisdiction over power developments on both the Ottawa and St. Lawrence rivers. This led him to take a strong stand on provincial rights in general. Quebec too wanted strong provincial powers to ensure the protection of French language rights and to enable it to sell power to Ontario. Once he had repealed Regulation 17, which had long been a sore point for Quebec, Ferguson was able to enlist Quebec's support. At a dominion–provincial conference on the constitution in 1927, Ferguson won his water rights. Along with the Quebec premier, he also insisted that the consent of all the provinces had to be obtained before the constitution could be amended, a demand which affected constitutional developments in Canada for many decades after.

By the time Ferguson turned over the Conservative government to George Henry in 1930, Ontario was a very different place than it had been when the United Farmers came to power in 1919. The decade had begun with the rural community making a last bid for continuing political dominance. With the collapse of the

UFO and the Ferguson government's active encouragement of diversified economic development, Ontario was looking by the end of the twenties towards a more urban and industrial future.

The Western Provinces

The situation was quite different in the west. In contrast to Ontario, the prairie population was still mostly rural (approximately 65 percent), so rural depopulation was not an issue. What the issues were, however, varied from one western province to another. Again, the disunity characteristic of the federal Progressives and the United Farmers of Ontario was evident in the diversity of views in the farmers' movements in the western provinces.

One of the few issues which united them was their opposition to the tariff and the groups which supported it. Whatever their other differences, this united western farmers against a common enemy, the "big vested interests"—the mostly eastern elite in the banks, the railways and the industrial sector, along with the traditional political parties which supported them. Added to this was the farmers' resentment of the marketing system for wheat. As prices fell in the early 1920s, farmers became more and more determined to establish a more equitable and reliable means of selling their wheat. Beyond these issues, however, the provincial organizations were quite different.

The United Farmers of Alberta (UFA) came to power in 1921. Henry Wise Wood was president of the UFA from 1916 to 1930. Because of his theory of group government, he was opposed to any direct political involvement on the part of the UFA. However, when it became clear that such involvement was inevitable, he advocated a rejection of the usual party structure and parliamentary system. He argued that the UFA should govern through co-operation rather than competition and confrontation. In other words it should try to establish a model group government and a solid base from which the farmers could defend their interests.

Like the UFO victory in 1919, the election of the UFA in 1921 was a surprise and the party found itself about to take power with no leader. Wood refused to be premier, although he remained a key adviser to the party. The government was led first by Herbert Greenfield (1921–1925), then by John Brownlee (1925–1934) and finally by R.G. Reid (1934–1935). In practice the UFA fell short of its radical theory. It was not easy to adapt the parliamentary system to group government. It was the UFA that adapted to the parliamentary system. Almost immediately, the government conformed to the established political structure, with leadership coming from the leader and the cabinet, and a secondary, purely supportive role assigned to the grassroots party and the backbenchers in the legislature.

IMMIGRATION AND THE KU KLUX KLAN

Immigration was a controversial issue in the 1920s. During the decade, an average of 120 000 people immigrated to Canada every year. Some native-born Canadians saw immigrants, particularly those who were not from Great Britain, as a threat and reacted to them with suspicion and hostility. But at the same time, economic expansion, particularly in the boom years in the middle of the decade, depended on cheap labour, a need that for the most part was met by "nonpreferred immigrants"— newcomers whose origins made them the targets of such prejudice.

Typically the King government tried to play both sides of the issue. In 1925, it adopted a liberal immigration policy to ensure that the growth of the labour force would keep pace with the rapid expansion of the economy. At the same time, it sought to offset the racist backlash against such open policies by launching massive campaigns to encourage the most preferred immigrants, the British. These campaigns were designed to appease racist sentiment by seeming to reinforce and protect Canada's Anglo-Saxon community. But such plans ran into problems of their own. The British often simply didn't stay. And many Canadians, especially those in government and business, objected strongly to the radical politics and trade union activism which British immigrants often brought with them.

As long as the nonpreferred immigrants were concentrated mainly in the more remote, newly developed parts of the country, racial and cultural tension remained at a relatively low level. But as immigrants, like other Canadians, began to move in greater and greater numbers to the cities, tension increased and the government restricted non-British immigration. By the end of the decade, with the economy faltering and unemployment on the rise, there was considerable opposition to any immigration, from Britain as well as from other countries. The result was policies from both the King and Bennett governments that brought immigration to a virtual halt through the Depression of the 1930s.

One of the more extreme groups exploiting such tensions in the twenties was the Ku Klux Klan (KKK), an American white supremacist organization. In the United States most of its actions were directed against Blacks, but when it moved northward into Canada in the twenties, the Klan took a wider aim, directing its hatred against anyone who was not white, English-speaking and Protestant. In addition to political campaigns, propaganda and its trade-mark cross-burnings, the Klan was suspected of more violent tactics, such as arson, raids and assault.

The Klan was active across Canada, but it was strongest in the west, where minority groups were either big enough or visible enough to be particularly vulnerable to discrimination. In British Columbia, the Klan joined in the attack on the Oriental communities. Although it formed a very

These Highland Scots are waiting at Tail-of-the-Bank, near Greenock, Scotland, to board the Canadian Pacific steamship Montrose. *They are bound for new homes in Vernon, British Columbia.*

Ku Klux Klan members outside their headquarters in Vancouver.

reduce the number of Japanese fishermen on the Pacific coast, on the grounds that they were driving white fishermen out of business.

By the mid-twenties the Klan had taken hold in Alberta, where their campaign was directed against central and eastern Europeans, and against the Roman Catholic French-Canadian minority. The Klan's propaganda blamed these groups for every social problem from unemployment to crime and insanity. They scored political successes in 1930 when two candidates they supported in the mayoral race and in the federal election were elected in Edmonton.

The Klan achieved its greatest successes in Saskatchewan where the most important factor in its success was its alliance with the provincial Conservative party. A number of prominent Conservatives were also leading members of the Klan. In the 1929 election, the Tories campaigned on some of the Klan's key issues: immigration and the use of French, particularly in schools. Their campaign, actively backed by the Klan, was successful and, once in power, the Tories did pass some anti-French legislation, including limitations on the use of French in education.

By the early 1930s, however, the Klan in Canada began to decline. Increasingly many of the minority groups it attacked, including French Canadians, Jews and Blacks, fought back through the press and political action. The Klan was further weakened by internal disagreements and scandals. Although still active as late as 1937, it was no longer a significant force in Canadian politics.

small part of the province's total population, the Japanese community was an easy target for the Klan because it was already the victim of harsh and widespread discrimination.

Union leaders also got into the act, and all too often, politicians as well shared these prejudices. In 1922 federal regulations were introduced to

A railway crew made up mainly of immigrant labourers.

The UFA, especially under Brownlee's leadership, provided practical, essentially conservative government. It did go some way towards meeting farmers' needs. Greenfield, Wood and Brownlee were all involved in the establishment of the Alberta Wheat Pool in 1923. In the same year the UFA introduced the Debt Adjustment Act to help farmers in financial difficulty. The government also improved railway service in northern Alberta, health care, education and the regulations governing the minimum wage and workers' compensation. One of the UFA's most important achievements was Brownlee's success with W.F.A. Turgeon, the attorney-general of Saskatchewan, in negotiating the transfer of control over crown lands and natural resources from federal to provincial jurisdiction.

In these ways, the UFA did give effective representation to western grievances and aspirations. By the mid-twenties, however, the radical farmers were beginning to be disappointed by the UFA's moderate policies. Their assistance to farmers did not go far enough to help the poorer farmers, and their cuts in government spending and the civil service put off those UFA supporters who wanted the state to take a more active role in the reform of the economic system. The party was further weakened when falling wheat prices caused the collapse of the Wheat Pool, which it had helped to create. By the mid-thirties, these problems had been aggravated by severe drought, the Depression, disagreements within the party and charges of personal scandal against Brownlee. In the 1935 election, the United Farmers were crushed by the Social Credit League led by William Aberhart. They lost all their seats in the legislature and ceased to play a direct role in Alberta politics.

In Manitoba the emergence of the United Farmers of Manitoba (UFM) as a political party was just as sudden and surprising as it had been in Alberta and Ontario. From 1915 to 1922 Manitoba was governed by a strong, progressive Liberal administration led by T.C. Norris. Under Norris's administration, women got the vote (1916), farmers received financial assistance, and industrial working conditions, workers' compensation and the minimum wage were improved. The Norris government introduced prohibition and provided some assistance for widows with children. There were also reforms in health and education and an active program of road construction and other publicly funded projects. Despite these expenditures, the Liberals were also able to eliminate the provincial debt.

Nonetheless, the momentum behind the farmers' protest movement was so strong that the tide began to turn against the Liberals. In 1920 the United Farmers elected twelve members to the legislature. In 1922 they were returned with a small majority and formed the government. Like the UFO and the UFA, their

Native People
The 1920s brought Canada's native people no relief from the discrimination, poverty and hardship which they had endured for so long. The decade did, however, see efforts by native people to organize themselves to fight for their rights. F.O. Loft, an Ontario Mohawk who had been an officer in the war, began to organize the League of Indians of Canada. In British Columbia, where no treaty or land settlement had ever been negotiated, the Allied Tribes of British Columbia, led by the Reverend Peter Kelly, a Haida, and Andrew Paull, a Squamish, struggled against the invasion of ancestral lands by miners, loggers and white settlers. The organization broke up in 1927 but the struggle was soon resumed by the Native Brotherhood of British Columbia, formed in 1931, and continues to this day.

Opposite page: Premier John Bracken (right) meets a delegation of native people at the Manitoba legislature in 1929 to negotiate resource rights.

Working on the Hudson Bay Railway in the early twenties. A railway connecting prairie wheat fields with Hudson Bay was first proposed in 1870, but work did not begin until 1906. Problems caused by muskeg, permafrost, economics and politicians repeatedly delayed the line's progress, and it finally reached the port of Churchill in 1929. The railway opened for commercial traffic two years later. Now part of the CNR, the line is still used for wheat shipments and for summer tourists.

appeal to the voters was based on a call to return to supposedly rural values—thrift, sobriety and hard work.

In practice the UFM did not implement radical agrarian reform. Under the conservative leadership of John Bracken, the UFM reduced public expenditure and trimmed the civil service to ensure a balanced provincial budget. In response to farmers' complaints about the wheat marketing system, especially the trade in futures on the Winnipeg Grain Exchange, Bracken's government set up the Manitoba Wheat Pool in 1924. During this period, there were also major industrial developments in Manitoba in mining, pulp and paper, and hydro-electric power. In 1924 Bracken joined the "On-to-the-Bay Association" to push the federal government to complete the long-delayed Hudson Bay Railway, which would serve the new resource industries in the province's northeast. These new industries signalled a transformation in the province's economy: by the end of the decade, the value of industrial output exceeded that of the agricultural sector.

The changing nature of the province's economy was reflected in the shift in Bracken's power base. In 1928 the UFM quit active politics and turned its energies to developing co-operative marketing systems and campaigning for reforms in transportation, banking and the tariff. Bracken turned away from farmers' politics and looked elsewhere for support. Over the next decade and a half, he held on to power through various alliances with the Liberals, Social Credit, Conservatives and the Co-operative Commonwealth Federation (CCF). In 1942 he left provincial politics to become the leader of the federal Conservative party—renamed the Progressive Conservative party at his insistence.

Farmers' unrest made itself felt in British Columbia and Saskatchewan too but in a less direct and dramatic way. The Liberals had been in power since Saskatchewan became a province in 1905, and they remained in office until 1929. The farm protest movement was very strong in Saskatchewan. In the 1921 federal election the Progressives took all but one of the province's seats in the House of Commons. But in provincial politics the farmers' influence made itself felt through the governing Liberals. The inclusion in the Liberal government of prominent farm leaders, most notably C.A. Dunning who was premier from 1922 to 1926, won the support of the chief farm organizations, the Saskatchewan Grain Growers' Association and the Saskatchewan Co-operative Elevator Company. Rather than pursuing political power itself, the farmers worked effectively with the Liberal government. One of their most important achievements was the establishment in 1924 of the Saskatchewan Wheat Pool to replace the existing unsatisfactory marketing system.

The Liberals were successful in containing the farm unrest that had caused such electoral upheavals in the two neighbouring provinces. Nonetheless, the Liberals were defeated in 1929. After more than twenty years in power, the party machine had grown too powerful. The voters rebelled against a variety of Liberal practices and policies, such as patronage appointments in the civil service and the government's road-building program. The Liberals were replaced by a coalition of Conservatives, Progressives and Independents headed by Dr. J.T.M. Anderson, an educator best known as a proponent of forceful assimilation of "foreigners."

Of the western provinces, British Columbia was in some respects the odd one out. Its agricultural work force was small compared to the other western provinces, and the types of crops were different. British Columbia's farmers were particularly dependent on growing fruits and vegetables for the Canadian market. It was in their interests to support tariffs protecting them from competing imports. Organizations such as the United Farmers of British Columbia and the B.C. Fruit Growers' Association had little in common with the prairie protest movements. Although farm protest did have some small impact in British Columbia, there was neither the population base nor the policy incentive to motivate direct political action.

There were significant developments in other areas of the economy, particularly in mining and forestry, in the 1920s. Shipping and shipbuilding had been increasingly important since the opening of the Panama Canal in 1914. The canal made European markets accessible to British Columbia, and the province's export trade continued to grow during the twenties.

For much of this period, from 1918 to 1927, British Columbia was governed by the Liberals led by John Oliver. Oliver was widely respected for his honesty if not his imagination. He provided steady leadership to British Columbia through the aftermath of the war and the economic downturn in the early twenties. He encouraged developments in fruit growing and marketing. He also pressed for the reform of federal transportation policy and tried to sort out the financial difficulties of the Pacific Great Eastern Railway, which would eventually—but not until 1955—link Vancouver to the northern interior of the province.

When Oliver died in 1927, he was succeeded by his finance minister, J.D. MacLean. Lacking Oliver's personal appeal, MacLean led his party to defeat in the 1928 election. The succeeding Conservative government under Simon Tolmie quickly fell apart because of party disunity and the catastrophic problems brought on by the Depression.

Maritime Rights

There was considerable unrest in the Maritime provinces in the 1920s, but as in British Columbia the farm protest movement was a relatively small part of it. Farm and labour candidates did do very well in the 1920 election in Nova Scotia, and the United Farmers' Party took six seats in New Brunswick in the same year. However, it was the Maritime Rights movement which was the real expression of protest in the eastern provinces in the 1920s.

The port of Vancouver was a key factor in British Columbia's prosperity in the twenties. As the global economy improved, British Columbia's trade across the Pacific and, through the Panama Canal, across the Atlantic increased so rapidly that the port's facilities were pushed to the limit to keep up with the volume of business.

The Maritime Rights movement was an economic protest. By 1918 the modest prosperity which the region had achieved during the war began to fail, and the decline continued right through the 1920s. The collapse of the economy was evident in virtually every aspect of Maritime life. The wealth generated by the manufacturing and resource industries declined drastically. The coal industry on which the region was so dependent was particularly hard hit by competition from new hydro-electric and oil developments in other parts of the country. Industrial towns shrank and emigration rose sharply as many Maritimers were forced to look for work elsewhere in Canada or in the United States.

The deterioration in the region's economy was greatly aggravated by tariff reforms which benefited central Canada at the expense of the Maritimes, and by protectionist measures in the United States which hurt the Maritimes' export trade in agricultural produce and fish. Even more damaging were changes in federal transportation policy. In 1918 the regional railway, the Intercolonial (ICR), which ran between Halifax and Montreal, was taken over by the Canadian National Railways (CNR). This meant that the railway's headquarters were in central Canada rather than Moncton where they had been. Huge rate increases followed; from 1918 to 1922, freight rates went up 111 percent. The effect on regional industry was catastrophic. Companies based in central Canada in many cases simply moved their operations out of the Maritimes. Without the ICR's protective freight rates, it was much more difficult for local enterprises to compete against goods produced elsewhere.

On top of these disastrous blows to the economy, the Maritime provinces found themselves with reduced representation in the House of Commons. The combination of political weakness, economic hardship and the region's traditional wariness about central Canada gave rise to the Maritime Rights movement. It had wide support across the region. Acadian and farm organizations, newspapers and trade unions were all involved. The leaders of the movement were mostly in business and the professions. Through local boards of trade, the movement's supporters revived a regional organization, the Maritime Board of Trade, to represent their views. Speeches were made across the country, conferences were held, representations were made to Ottawa and pamphlets were published. The movement wanted increased subsidies from the federal government, a new transportation policy that would restore favourable freight rates and encourage use of Maritime ports, and tariffs to protect the coal and steel industries.

The Maritime Rights movement worked through the existing political parties rather than trying to mount a third-party challenge as the farm protest organizations had. As a result, much of the political activity in the Maritimes in the 1920s both federally and provincially had to do with the Liberals and Conservatives jockeying for the votes of Maritime Rights supporters. The federal Conservatives started the decade at a disadvantage because their government had been responsible for the CNR's takeover of the ICR. In the 1921 federal election, the Liberals took all but six Maritime seats in the Commons. The provincial Tories had already been crushed in Prince Edward Island in 1919, and in Nova Scotia and New Brunswick in 1920.

The failure of the federal Liberal government to address Maritime concerns once it was in power gave the Tories a new opportunity. Maritime Rights became the vehicle by which the federal and provincial Tories rebuilt their power base in the region. Although Meighen made no specific commitments, the Tories' efforts to present themselves as the defenders of Maritime Rights paid off. They returned to power in Prince Edward Island in 1923, taking all but five seats in the provincial legislature. In the 1925 election in Nova Scotia, they defeated the Liberals who had been in power in the province for forty-three years without a break. In the same year, New Brunswick opted strongly for a Conservative government.

Not surprisingly, this massive swing to the Tories carried over into the federal election in 1925. The scale of the Conservative gains in the region finally forced King to recognize the strength of the Maritime Rights movement. Early in 1926, the federal government appointed a royal commission to look into Maritime grievances. Despite this bid for Maritime support, the Liberals did only slightly better in the region in the 1926 election.

The Royal Commission on Maritime Claims was chaired by a British lawyer, Sir Andrew Rae Duncan, and it was a serious attempt to come up with some solutions to the very real dilemmas facing the Maritime provinces. It recommended a 20 percent reduction in rail rates, help for Atlantic ports and for the steel and coal industries, and increased federal subsidies for all three provinces. The report was received with tremendous enthusiasm in the Maritimes, but the federal government responded cautiously to its demands. There were some reductions in rail rates and some incentives were provided to encourage the sale of Nova Scotia's coal. But many of the commission's recommendations were ignored. For the most part, the King government went only as far as it felt it had to to protect its own political interests. The Maritime provinces went on to face the same problems to a far more serious degree in the Depression of the 1930s.

Quebec

After the First World War, Quebec was more acutely aware than ever of its differences from the other provinces. Many English Canadians emerged from the war with a new sense of Canada's national identity, but this was not shared by French Canadians. The conscription crisis had left Quebec distrustful of the federal government. Laws curtailing the teaching of French in Manitoba and Ontario schools led many Quebeckers to believe that their language and culture were not respected elsewhere in the country. This uneasiness was demonstrated in 1918 when the Quebec Assembly debated the issue of the province's relationship with the rest of Canada: " . . . this House . . . would be disposed to accept the breaking of the Confederation Act of 1867 if, in the other provinces, it is believed that she is an obstacle to the union, progress and development of Canada." After long discussion, in which not a single speaker favoured secession, the motion was withdrawn. Nonetheless, the isolation of Canada's two cultures from one another was more than usually pronounced during the twenties.

Of all the institutions fundamental to French-speaking society in Quebec, none was more important than the Roman Catholic Church. The church took a leading role in the development of a conservative nationalism intended to defend the French language and culture in Quebec, and to protect it from modern, secular influences from outside the province. Most priests and church leaders in Quebec encouraged their parishioners to cling to the traditions of a simple agricultural life. Rural life was considered morally superior to the cold and impersonal materialism of industrial cities like Montreal. The culture of Quebec could not survive in the city, the church preached. Only in the countryside would Quebec's language and religion be secure.

A leading Quebec historian and cleric of the time, Lionel Groulx, put the idea in simple terms. "We must sow or go jobless, our people must be agricultural or perish." Groulx's conservative, Catholic nationalism was an important influence in Quebec in the 1920s. From 1920 to 1928, he edited a monthly journal and spearheaded a political movement, both called *Action Française*. His nationalism focused on Quebec's traditional values and religion, and the interpretation of its history as a struggle for cultural, religious and linguistic survival. Groulx did his best to discourage films, books and magazines from outside Quebec.

In contrast to the isolationist tendency in Groulx's thought, nationalist politician and writer Henri Bourassa was committed to the idea of a bicultural Canada in which English and French would have equal status. But Bourassa did share something of Groulx's distrust of modern industrial society, and he was particularly concerned with the survival of Quebec's Catholic values. He even saw a unique religious role for his people: "Our special

Historian, priest and nationalist, Lionel-Adolphe Groulx is often considered the spiritual father of modern Quebec.

task, as French Canadians, is to insert into America the spirit of Christian France. It is to defend against all comers, perhaps even against France herself, our religious and national heritage . . . it is the refuge and fortress and anchor amid the immense sea of saxonizing Americanism.''

The call to the land echoed across the province, but the trend to the city continued. As in the rest of Canada, the population of Quebec was becoming increasingly urbanized during the twenties. The Liberal government headed by Louis-Alexandre Taschereau, which was in power from 1920 to 1936, did everything it could to encourage the modernization of Quebec. In addition to reforms in education and social policy, Taschereau promoted industrial growth and sought out foreign investment to develop Quebec's natural resources. At the same time, he did not want the province to become too heavily urbanized. Therefore, he encouraged industries to come to the small communities in Quebec, rather than to larger centres. Taschereau wrote, ''In the transition from agricultural village to company town the parish priest would care for his parishioners as always. The populations affected would see their pattern of employment shift from agricultural to industrial work, their incomes would rise, and all such benefits would occur without their leaving home.'' Taschereau was a strong defender of Quebec's constitutional claims, but his moderate views on confederation and his policies favouring development and modernization set him at odds with nationalists such as Groulx and Bourassa. Although the conservative nationalists seemed to be the dominant voice in Quebec during the twenties, the social and economic forces which Taschereau's policies encouraged were bringing about significant changes in Quebec society.

Even in union organization, church influence was strong in Quebec during the twenties. In 1921, the church-sponsored Confédération de travailleurs catholiques du Canada (CTCC) was formed. It was a Catholic union representing the small number of Quebec workers who were organized. Although the CTCC had conservative beginnings, it gradually became more radical, especially after a particularly bitter strike in the shoe industry in Quebec City in 1926. However, the growth of unions in the province did not keep pace with industrialization. The work force continued to be made up mostly of underpaid, unorganized workers. Low wages and long working hours helped to attract foreign investment, mostly American, and led to a sharp growth of industry in centres such as Trois-Rivières, Hull, Shawinigan, Grand-Mère, Chicoutimi, La Tuque and Montreal. Quebec was turning into a predominantly urban society.

For many years, Thérèse Casgrain led the Quebec women's struggle for the vote and other rights. When the suffrage movement in Quebec split into two groups in 1927, Casgrain emerged as the leader of the League for Women's Rights. After the vote was finally won in 1940, Casgrain continued to fight for a wide range of social and political reforms. An active member of the Co-operative Commonwealth Federation, she was the first woman in Canada to lead a political party when she became the leader of the Quebec wing of the CCF in 1951.

REVIEW AND DISCUSSION

Key People and Ideas
Explain the importance of each of the following as they are discussed in the chapter.

Ernest C. Drury
Howard Ferguson
Henry Wise Wood
John Brownlee
John Bracken
J.T.M. Anderson
John Oliver
Sir Andrew Rae Duncan
Lionel Groulx

Henri Bourassa
Louis-Alexandre Taschereau
Thérèse Casgrain
Regulation 17
Fergie's Foam
The Debt Adjustment Act
The "On-to-the-Bay" Association
The B.C. Fruit Growers' Association
Confédération de travailleurs
catholiques du Canada

Analysing the Issues
Answer each of the following questions, which deal with important issues raised in the chapter.

1. How did rural depopulation affect politics and society in the 1920s?
2. How effective was the Royal Commission on Maritime Claims?
3. In what ways did Lionel Groulx, Louis-Alexandre Taschereau and Henri Bourassa differ in their attitudes towards Quebec's future?

Questions for Discussion
Think carefully about each of the following questions and discuss the issues which they raise.

1. Farmers' political parties were active across the country in the 1920s. What were their differences and similarities from one province to another? Did they succeed in what they set out to do?
2. What were the main developments in federal–provincial relations in the 1920s? Do you think that the relationship between Ottawa and the provinces is better or worse now than it was in the twenties?

4

WHEAT: BOOM AND BUST

During the twenties, more of the prairie population farmed than at any time before or since. Heavy ploughs, harnessing as many as sixteen horses, efficiently turned thick, age-old sod into fertile seed-beds for the new, hardy grain provided by scientific agriculture. As soon as the snow melted, heavy gang ploughs snaked their way across the fields, followed by harrows smoothing the seed-beds. Immense seed drills would then score their way across the treeless farms.

Wheat was the chief prairie grain. Spring wheat—hard red wheat—was in demand throughout the western world because it was rich in protein. Once ground into flour, it allowed bakers to produce a large, light loaf of bread under a variety of baking conditions. Thus European bakers coveted Canadian wheat to mix with their home-grown varieties, which by themselves produced small, heavy loaves.

After soaring to new heights in 1919—persuading tens of thousands of war veterans to plough their savings into becoming wheat farmers—the price of grain tumbled faster than it had risen. By 1921, wheat was 80¢ a bushel, down from $2.45 in 1918. That was better than the disastrous 66¢ of 1913—but inflation had halved the value of a dollar.

Reasons were not hard to find. The grain producing regions of central Europe were back in business by 1921 and European countries no longer had to look across the Atlantic for food supplies. Australia and Argentina entered the world grain markets with bumper crops, adding to supply and driving prices down. Over the decade, there was a slow recovery in prices but the lasting damage to prairie soil from almost a generation of grain mining could not be repaired. When dry years came in the 1930s, farmers and all Canadians paid a terrible price for environmental neglect.

Mechanization of Agriculture

Mechanization of agriculture was slow during the early twenties. In 1921, 86 percent of prairie farmers used horses, and only 38 000 tractors were in use. But sales increased as the decade went on and wheat prices improved. By 1930, there were 85 000 tractors on Canada's farms.

The early gasoline-driven tractors cost twice as much as Model T Fords, which competed for the farmers' dollars. Tractors came in a bewildering assortment of makes and models. One writer estimated that there were seventy-five manufacturers trying to sell farm tractors in 1920, and some of these companies had three or four models. Their unreliability forced many farmers to resort to horses in the middle of spring ploughing or fall harvesting. Tractors were often abandoned to rust in forgotten fence-rows as farmers turned back to horse-drawn discs,

Opposite page:
The first contracts of the Saskatchewan Wheat Pool, following its establishment in 1924. The Wheat Pools set up in the prairie provinces in the twenties allowed farmers to sell their grain co-operatively. Returns from grain sales were "pooled," expenses deducted, and the profits divided among all those who had contracts with the Pool.

The manufacturers of farm
equipment used every
conceivable sales pitch to
promote mechanized
farming. Farm journals
and magazines were filled
with success stories,
photographs, statistics and
even jokes, such as this one
from Canadian Tractor
Farming:

Visitor: "Can you spell
horse?"

Hostess' Little Girl: "I
could if I wanted to, but
what's the use of spellin'
anything so out of
style?"

ploughs and harrows. But the need for more efficient machinery remained and new tractor models continued to lure farmers, even though the investment put them into debt. The February 3, 1927 issue of *Farm and Dairy* published an article documenting farmers' experience with tractors. Four out of five considered their tractors a paying investment:

> The tractor enables the work to be done more quickly in the spring and thereby secures somewhat larger yields. It also enables the land to be plowed in the summer and cultivated during the fall so as to permit more thorough eradication of weeds. With such weeds as couch grass, the land should be worked when it is dry and when the weather is hot. The tractor is very useful under such conditions.

Tractors did more than improve crop yields. Of at least equal importance was the reduction in the number of hired hands a farmer needed if he had a tractor. The belt power of a forty-five horsepower tractor could drive corn-cutting machines to fill silos, power larger and larger threshing machines and provide the turning motion for innumerable portable saws that cut firewood into blocks for splitting.

There were, however, farmers who continued to prefer horses, complaining that tractors were too expensive, wasteful and noisy. They destroyed the peace of country life. "I always preferred the horses," said Elsie Freeman's brother, "because they had to rest every once in a while, which gave me a break at the same time. With tractors there was no rest."

Whatever their preferences, farmers, like their city cousins were interested in profits. When reliable tractors became available in large numbers at low prices, even the most reluctant converted. In 1927, a farm association concluded that tractors lasted an average of 12.38 years. Pro-rating the purchase price and the cost of repairs, fuel and oil on the basis of an average of just over fifty days use per year, it estimated that the cost of a tractor worked out to $5.62 per day of use. A driver was paid $3.00 a day, which brought the total daily cost of running a tractor to $8.62. This was significantly less than it would cost to pay and feed the number of farm hands and maintain the number of horses needed to accomplish the same amount of work. The farm horse was doomed—though it did make a brief reappearance on the bankrupt farms of the Depression-torn thirties.

With the tractor, however, the farmer became more tightly bound to the industrial heartland of Canada, a link that bred both dependence and resentment. The eastern farm-implement industry that produced tractors was protected by tariffs, while

western farmers had to sell their grain on an open world market. As grain prices fell during the twenties, the resentment of western farmers against tariff restrictions increased.

The Tariff

The grievances of western farmers were well summed up in an editorial from a 1924 issue of the magazine *Canadian Forum*:

> High transportation charges, to be blamed on the eastern-controlled railroads; high rates of interest, due to eastern banking and investing methods; high cost of production, chargeable to the eastern manufacturer and protectionist, who maintain the outrageously high tariff on implements and other necessities—these combine to keep the prairie farmer on the brink of financial collapse.

Of all grievances, the tariff was pre-eminent. Tariffs made good sense to eastern manufacturers, who feared they would be unable to stay in business if foreign goods, principally American, were allowed to compete freely in the Canadian market. Cheap

A typical advertisement for farm machinery from the Grain Growers' Guide for March 1921. Mechanization revolutionized farming in the 1920s, and in their advertising manufacturers regularly stressed how farm machinery, with its greater speed and cost efficiency, was making the use of horses obsolete.

American products could destroy Canadian industry. Workers would be hurt as much as manufacturers. And there were some farmers, including Ontario grape growers, British Columbia fruit growers, and dairy farmers in Quebec and the Maritimes, who wanted tariff protection from competing American agricultural producers.

However, the anti-tariff forces included many farmers all across the country. They argued that the removal of the tariff would bring farmers back to the land. Access to cheaper American farm machinery would keep their costs down and allow them to make a necessary margin of profit on their farms. Western farmers felt particularly strongly on the subject since heavy transportation costs were added to the already higher prices of Canadian-made machinery.

Moreover, while farming on the prairies could be very profitable, it was also very risky. Eastern farms were sufficiently diversified that a disaster was never total. But prairie farms were basically dependent on one crop—and one that had to be sold. If wheat prices dropped, families could not survive on their wheat, no matter how many hundreds of bushels of it they had. And if an early frost, disease, drought or insects wiped out the wheat crop, they did not have potatoes or apples or dairy herds to fall back on. The extra cost of Canadian-made farm machinery and other tariff-protected manufactured goods could mean the difference between profit or at least breaking even and going into debt—if not into bankruptcy. Getting rid of the tariff, however, required more political clout and unity than farmers would ever have again.

The Formation of Wheat Pools

There is, so the saying goes, more than one way to skin a cat. If western farmers could not get rid of the tariff and lower their costs, could they do something to ensure good prices for their wheat? They certainly could, claimed Aaron Sapiro, an American farm organizer who travelled through western Canada in the early twenties making stirring speeches about the benefits that would flow if only farmers formed co-operatives, or *pools,* to collectively store and market their wheat. According to Sapiro:

> The central problem of the farm is to try to stop dumping by the farmers. Every farmer in the world who sells as an individual is dumping his product . . . . The fundamental thing is to stop the dumping of farm products, stop individual selling, stop local selling, and organize the commodity on such a plan that you will sell a great portion of that commodity from one office on a straight merchandising plan. By merchan-

Opposite page:
George Black (left) of Ayr, Ontario, was the kind of farmer who welcomed technological change, whether it was a car for his family (top) or machinery for his farm. In the lower picture, he and his neighbours use a stationary gas engine to cut firewood. Black loved machines. He even invented a windmill that was built on top of his barn and could be used to drive a grain grinder, a wood lathe and a planing machine to dress lumber.

dising, we mean control the flow of any given commodity, so that it goes to the markets of the world, wherever they are, in such times, and in such quantities that they will be absorbed at a price that is fair.

In other words, co-operative action could be the answer. Western farmers listened eagerly, and by the mid-twenties, Sapiro's work had led to the formation of the prairie Wheat Pools, whose towering storage elevators soon came to symbolize the united purpose of prairie farmers. The Alberta Wheat Pool was organized in 1923 and the Saskatchewan and Manitoba Wheat Pools in 1924.

From the mid-twenties, the Wheat Pools aggressively marketed the prairie wheat crops and procured higher prices for western farmers. Payment was regular—a down payment when wheat was delivered, and the balance in regular instalments determined by the price that the Wheat Pool got for the wheat crop. The pools also distracted farmers from politics and social reform. They could get rich like other capitalists who could "corner a market"—or they could if prices kept climbing. When they fell, as in late 1928, other rules took over. But always in the west, "Next year will be better."

The years from 1924 to 1929 were golden ones for western wheat growers. As long as world demand for wheat exceeded supply, the Wheat Pools were a striking success. The price of wheat on the Winnipeg Grain Exchange rocketed upward from $1.25 a bushel in 1924 to $2.20 in the spring of 1925. The price dropped after that, but while yields remained high and the market held, farmers who were content to grow and sell their wheat pros-

Threshing crew, near Milestone, Saskatchewan, 1926. Threshing gangs cut and bound sheaves of grain into stooks, then hauled these stooks to giant stationary threshing machines. These machines were powered by long-drive belts attached to steam-driven tractors.

pered. But for those who acquired a taste for speculating, this prosperity had its risks.

Gambling on the Winnipeg Grain Exchange

The Winnipeg Grain Exchange was the central selling point for prairie wheat. As farmers and others with a stake in agriculture invested their profits, the Exchange came to resemble a giant gambling hall. For a time during the 1920s, the Winnipeg Grain Exchange was the largest office building in the British Empire. It had a smoking room, cuspidors (spittoons), a billiard room, slot machines and space for the offices of all wheat speculators, from the owners of grain elevator companies to representatives of millers, exporters and American corporate giants.

The "pit" was located on the sixth floor of the Exchange. Actually, there were two pits, one for wheat and the other for coarse grains such as oats, barley and rye. Wheat brokers milled about the pit, while Exchange employees entered grain prices on the blackboard above the trading floor. Telegraph link-ups and banks of telephones relayed information to and from similar exchanges in New York, Chicago, Liverpool, Minneapolis and Duluth. Winnipeg was wired to the wider world and was the centre of all grain speculation in the west. The information from Winnipeg was eagerly picked up by farmers across the west listening with strained ears through the headphones of crystal sets (early, often homemade radios). The few commercial radio stations always broadcast grain prices as a leading news item.

The action on the Winnipeg Grain Exchange was seasonal: periods of frantic activity in the spring and summer, when speculation about the size of the harvest was at a peak, followed by

periods of slower activity, as the harvest increased the supply of grain, and then a quiet winter, when the Winnipeg Grain Exchange was silent and largely empty.

In 1923, farmers had a bumper crop. Over 452 million bushels of grain were delivered to the storage elevators that rose like giants across the prairie horizon. It was the best crop since 1915, with an average yield of 43 bushels to the acre (0.4 ha). Bumper crops have a dark side, however, because they yield lower prices—a kind of penalty for success. By comparison, the 1924 crop was disappointing—some 235 million bushels. But the price was good at $1.35 per bushel.

As news of a general crop failure elsewhere in the world percolated through the Winnipeg Grain Exchange, a wave of speculative buying began. The Exchange increased its activity that winter. By January 1925, the price of wheat had increased to $1.75 and seemed on its way to the magical figure of $2.00 per bushel. Gambling became epidemic. On Friday, January 13, 1925, the price passed $2.00 and the wheat pit was swarming with activity usually only seen in the summer. From winter to spring, as news of a serious drought in the Soviet Union circulated, the price continued to rise until it reached $2.20 per bushel.

The old saying, "What goes up must come down," is as true for speculative investments as for anything else. On May 29, 1925, the price of wheat began to drop. In fifteen minutes it plunged from $2.20 to $2.10, triggering a general downward trend. Soon it sank below $2.00. For the rest of the decade and into the next, the price of wheat continued to fall, reaching a low of 38 cents per bushel in 1931. Speculators who had bought while the price was still high found themselves deeply in debt.

CASH INCOME FROM WHEAT

Million dollars

Calendar year	Man.	Sask.	Alta.	Total
1926	41.6	240.3	107.4	389.3
1927	31.8	216.3	116.7	364.8
1928	34.4	256.4	149.9	440.7
1929	29.3	184.3	110.0	323.6
1930	19.3	86.8	52.6	158.7
1931	9.3	44.2	38.6	92.1

Farmers who speculated had to find a way to get to Winnipeg in the summer, look for a cheap hotel and then spend a few days in an option broker's office gambling in wheat. The broker

would in turn move upstairs to the pit to do the large-scale trading. Here is an imaginary scenario of a farmer speculating at the Exchange:

James Edwards plants his crop in the spring on his quarter section of land near Moosejaw, Saskatchewan. In early July, he persuades his family that a visit to Winnipeg is necessary. They don't need much persuasion. They have converted their farming operation from mixed farming to specialized wheat production, so they don't have that much to do at this time of year other than harrow down the weeds on the fallow acreage. They have time for a trip to the city while they are waiting through the long, hot summer for the frenzied activity of the fall harvest.

Once in town, James immediately visits the Winnipeg Grain Exchange and finds his broker's office. The broker allows him to buy wheat futures "on margin," which means he can buy a bushel of wheat with a down payment that is only a percentage of its real value. If the price is $1.00 a bushel and the margin is 10 percent, he can buy $1000 worth of wheat futures for $100—or a dollar's worth for ten cents. Occasionally the margin was higher—up to 50 percent of the value. The futures market is based on the idea that the value of wheat will increase. By purchasing wheat futures in July—that is, wheat that has not yet come to market and is either stored in elevators or still growing in the fields—it might be possible to make a quick profit as soon as the price starts to rise.

Margin buying increases the risk but also increases

Like the horse, cook cars for harvesting crews (from right to left, dining room, kitchen, water tank and fresh milk "factory") were almost obsolete by the end of the twenties. They made a brief comeback during the Depression when many farmers, no longer able to afford machinery, went back to working with horses and large crews of labourers.

the potential profit. James Edwards is a farmer, eternally optimistic that the next crop will be better than the last, that next year's price will be higher. Optimists make good gamblers.

James takes a seat in the broker's office and waits. If the price of grain rises one cent per bushel, then James makes $10. But suppose the price of grain increases by ten cents per bushel. James doubles his money. He may then pocket his profit and return to Moosejaw, after paying a 2.5 percent commission to his broker. Or, anticipating a steady increase in the price of wheat because of rumours of a drought in Australia or a grasshopper infestation in Manitoba, he can leave his money with his broker to be reinvested.

But what happened to speculators if, as was actually the case in the later twenties, the price of grain fell rather than rose? Let's look again at James Edwards's investment.

In 1925, James Edwards invests $100 in wheat at $2.20 per bushel. He buys on a 10 percent margin, so he owns 455 bushels of wheat futures—$1000 worth of wheat—for which he owes his broker $900. If the price falls and he can only sell the wheat at $2.00 a bushel, he will get $910 for it, that is just $10 more than he owes. Since he paid out $100 to buy the wheat futures in the first place, he takes a loss of $90—90 percent of his original investment.

Suppose James Edwards refuses to sell his wheat when the price starts to fall in 1925. He has to borrow money to pay in full for the 455 bushels. If he finally sells the grain stock in 1930 when the price is 55 cents a bushel, he gets only $250.25—out of his original investment of $1000. He loses not just the first hundred dollars but a total of $749.75.

Very few speculators were content with the kind of nickel and dime gambling that the imaginary James Edwards's loss represents. Most of them were in much deeper—ten, twenty, a hundred times deeper. And the crash, when it came, hit them a hundred times harder.

REVIEW AND DISCUSSION

Key People and Ideas
Explain the importance of each of the following as they are discussed in the chapter.

Aaron Sapiro	Wheat Pools
Spring Wheat	Winnipeg Grain Exchange
Tractors	
The tariff	

Analysing the Issues
Answer each of the following questions, which deal with important issues raised in the chapter.

1. In what ways did typical farm life begin to change during the twenties?
2. Why was the co-operative movement so successful on the prairies?
3. What were the risks of "margin buying"?
4. How did federal transportation policies affect western farmers?

Questions for Discussion
Think carefully about each of the following questions and discuss the issues which they raise.

1. Western farmers had a very different attitude towards the tariff than did eastern workers. What were the reasons for this and what does it tell us about Canada in the 1920s? Can you think of any parallels today?
2. The prairie economy in the twenties depended almost entirely on wheat. What were the consequences of this for farmers as the decade went on?

5

LABOUR:
A DISAPPOINTING DECADE

Elsie Freeman was not an exception when she packed her bag and moved from the family farm to Toronto. She was part of a great mass movement of Canadians from farms across the country to the growing industrial centres.

Why were the cities so attractive? There was a feeling of excitement in Canadian cities in the twenties. Electric lights brightened the night and leisure was no longer dictated by the movements of the sun. Cars, radios, paved streets, indoor plumbing, plays, books and baseball games all contributed to the conviction that the city was the place to be. Perhaps the city's greatest attraction was the chance to be part of the twentieth-century industrial awakening: to escape the routine of farm life, to get a good job with fixed hours, maybe to make it big.

Many young people flocking to the cities from the farms to join the burgeoning working class were looking for adventure. Most of them were quite prepared to accept long working hours, low pay, lay-offs, crowded living conditions and a high cost of living in order to establish themselves in the city. Unfortunately, the life they found there often remained a very hard one. Popular magazines and annuals may have given the impression of wide-spread wealth, but few workers were able to buy big cars, fancy clothes or motorboats. Many were badly fed and overworked.

Union Movements

Many migrants to the cities showed no interest in getting involved in the union movement. Nevertheless, the twenties were full of political action for labour—there was even considerable union activity in the garment trade both in Toronto and Montreal, although Elsie Freeman seems to have been unaware of it. The two major unions in the garment industry, the Amalgamated Clothing Workers (ACW) and the International Ladies Garment Workers Union (ILGWU), spent much of the decade locked in conflict between Communist and non-Communist organizers.

Out of the 1919 Winnipeg General Strike had emerged labour leaders who were deeply concerned about the exploitation of the urban working class. J.S. Woodsworth, Rev. William Irvine and A.A. Heaps, for example, sat on the Committee on Industrial and International Relations, established through the International Labour Organization of the League of Nations to direct attention to workers around the world. Their investigations caused deep concern among committee members, but they found it "almost impossible to shake the complacency of the middle class and rural born, whose solution to poverty was harder work and longer hours."

Evidence of the need for welfare policies to break the poverty cycle seemed to fall on deaf ears. Even demands for a minimum

Opposite page: *Miners Houses, Glace Bay,* by Lawren Harris, one of the painters in the Group of Seven. The strikes in the Cape Breton coal industry in the 1920s were long and bitter. In this 1925 painting, Harris, who visited Cape Breton in 1921, depicts the grim and barren world of the region's mining towns.

The first old-age
pension cheque was
issued in 1927 to W.H.
Derby (left) of British
Columbia.

NEGOTIABLE WITHOUT CHARGE AT ANY BRANCH OF ANY CHARTERED BANK OF BRITISH COLUMBIA

THE WORKMEN'S COMPENSATION BOARD   NO. 1. -

PRESENTED WITHIN THIRTY DAYS FROM DATE

CLAIM No.   VANCOUVER, B.C.
A-L $. 20.00   Sept. 20. 1927
William Henry Derby
PAY TO THE ORDER OF   Alberni, B.C.

THE SUM OF   Twenty Dollars.

                              THE WORKMEN'S COMPEPSATION BOARD

To
THE CANADIAN BANK OF COMMERCE   OLD AGE
VANCOUVER, B.C.   PENSIONS
                                  DEPARTMENT

wage were hard to root. It took two decades for some of these
policies to become law.

Nonetheless, under J.S. Woodsworth's influence, Labour
members without hidden Liberal or Tory ties sat in Parliament
for the first time ever. In this period mothers' allowances, blind
persons' allowances, the national employment service, and old-
age pensions got started. Unemployment insurance and family
allowances were extensively debated and sometimes promised.

The provinces were responsible for most of the innovations. Mother's allowances, minimum wages for women workers and stricter laws for the protection of children were a result of women's new political power at the ballot box.

Those Canadian workers who did belong to unions were divided into two groups: skilled and unskilled. The earliest unions were craft unions, composed of skilled craftsmen such as carpenters and leather workers. Large factories employed a variety of such workers and therefore had to deal with a number of unions. Employers were sometimes able to divide and conquer by playing off one union against another, but the general result of unionization was rising wages for skilled workers, who were often in great demand and short supply.

Unskilled workers, however, were more easily exploited by their employers and were looked down on by the craft union members with whom they worked. Since they had no special skills and could not join the craft unions, they began to support industrial unions—unions to which all the workers in an industry could belong no matter what jobs they held, skilled or unskilled. The Canadian Brotherhood of Railway Employees, for instance, included skilled workers such as mechanics as well as unskilled workers such as freight handlers.

The early 1920s were years of struggle between the newly-formed One Big Union (OBU) and the Trades and Labour Congress (TLC), an older organization. Both sought to control the labour movement and raided each other's membership. The TLC contained most of the craft unions and represented the newer American-based international unions. By contrast the OBU was distinctly Canadian. Bad economic times in the early twenties did not help unions in either organization, as membership fell and union funds declined. The OBU ultimately came out the loser. Under attack by the TLC and its international craft unions, the OBU leadership became increasingly fragmented. By 1923 the OBU had lost most of its membership. By 1926 many of the Canadian unions had regrouped into the All-Canadian Congress of Labour (ACCL) led by Aaron Mosher, and the campaign against the TLC and its American-based affiliates was renewed.

The leading advocate for the cause of industrial unions was R.B. Russell, a labour leader during the Winnipeg General Strike and chief representative of the OBU. When the OBU was organized during the Winnipeg General Strike, its constitution had announced that the Marxist class struggle was inevitable. It had urged Canadian workers to prepare "for the day when production for profit [would] be replaced by production for use." These words sounded revolutionary when coupled with newspaper headlines reporting the excesses of the Russian Revolution. Fear of communism, or "bolshevism," led to attacks on union organi-

The Communist Party of Canada was founded in 1921 in a barn near Guelph, Ontario. Its early meetings were secret because the War Measures Act, making the party illegal, was still in effect. When it became a legal political party in 1924, it changed its name from the Workers' Party of Canada to the Communist Party of Canada. Its membership came from Marxist parties loyal to the Soviet-dominated Communist International. Plagued by party infighting, the Communists also encountered obstacles in their attempts to gain influence in the labour movement. Initially, their strategy was to infiltrate the Trades and Labour Congress, but in 1927 they decided to form their own union, the Workers' Unity League (WUL). Government surveillance was close right from the start. Official hostility took many forms—meetings were broken up, offices raided and hundreds of foreign-born suspected communists were deported.

These coal miners were responsible for opening the shaft into a new coal seam. They worked in conditions that were usually cramped, wet and dangerous.

zers as well as discrimination against "foreigners." Eastern European immigrants in particular were considered closely linked to the Bolsheviks, even though many were actually refugees from the Russian Revolution.

J.S. Woodsworth, as Labour's parliamentary spokesman, had no love for communism but he knew that mere anti-communism was a distraction. "What is the subject of greatest interest to Labour men today?" Woodsworth asked a worker that year. "The coming winter," was the terse answer. Most workers were concerned with feeding and sheltering their families, and none were more concerned than the miners and steelworkers of Cape Breton where labour was involved in bitter and violent confrontations in the twenties.

The Cape Breton Coal Strike

The weakness of the labour movement through the twenties was tragically apparent in Cape Breton. There, in the first half of the decade, miners and steelworkers squared off against the owners of the Nova Scotia coal and steel industry in a series of bitter strikes. J.S. Woodsworth wrote in *Canadian Forum*:

> What is the root of all this trouble in Nova Scotia? Bolshevism among the foreign miners? No, that is not an adequate answer, though an easy way of disposing of any industrial difficulty. The miners in Nova Scotia are chiefly of Scotch-Canadian stock and there was similar trouble long before Lenin came upon the international stage. No case can be summed up in a word, yet there is one word that is much nearer than *Bolshevism*; that is *BESCO*.

BESCO—the British Empire Steel Corporation—owned all the coal mines and steel mills of Nova Scotia. It also owned the homes, stores, electrical and water systems, schools and social centres of the bleak mining towns scattered among the blackened collieries of Cape Breton. In 1920, a royal commission conluded that living and sanitary conditions were, with few exceptions, "absolutely wretched."

During the war, the demand for steel and coal allowed the wages of Cape Breton workers to be raised as their employer made vastly improved profits. With the war over, steel and coal prices, and hence profits, tumbled. BESCO president, Roy Wolvin, faced with cutting operations or cutting costs, chose the latter. Late in 1921, he announced a 33 percent cut in all labour rates.

The United Mineworkers had won a long, bitter struggle to represent the Cape Breton miners in 1917. Faced with the wage cut, the union ordered a slowdown which escalated, on August 14, 1922, to a walkout. Twelve thousand miners left their jobs at midnight. With them went maintenance workers and the miners who maintained the water pumps that kept the sea from flooding the deep underwater seams. A long strike spelled potential disaster. Cape Breton magistrates summoned 1200 soldiers— most of Canada's peace-time army—but even their presence could not force the miners back to work. Finally, Mackenzie King persuaded Wolvin to reduce the pay cut to 18 percent and the workers went back.

That was not the end of the story. The compromise was denounced by more radical miners. Silby Barrett, the Newfound-

Discrimination
An all-too-common attitude to "foreigners" was aptly summarized in 1925 by the Saskatchewan Minister of Public Health, J.M. Ulrich:
"If anybody teaches his children another language besides English, goes to his own church, drives an ox-team, paints Easter eggs, eats pea soup, bakes bread in a clay oven . . . faddist Canadianisers see a monstrous foreign menace raising its hideous head in the form of Easter eggs and clay ovens."

THE MILITANT COAL MINERS

The Coal Barons: "Trouble with you people is, you want the earth."
The Coal Miners: "Trouble with you is you've got it."

This cartoon expresses the bitter sense of exploitation which motivated the coal miners' struggle against BESCO. Its message is much the same as the call to radical action which J.B. McLachlan repeated again and again to the miners: "This land is yours, all yours, and you should own it and work it. You are doing the work and the capitalists are getting the riches."

lander who led the union, was accused of selling out his members. A fiery Scottish-born radical, James Bryson McLachlan, had been one of the pioneering union members on Cape Breton. McLachlan defeated Barrett in union elections and promised a more militant style. Typical of this was his reaction to the tragic case of Frank McIntyre, a miner with nine children and a sick wife. When the company store refused to give McIntyre more credit, he stole some flour, butter and sugar. He was arrested, taken to court in chains and sentenced to two years in jail. McLachlan raged in print that "a judge is a capitalist politician who is put upon the bench because he has faithfully served the capitalists as a politician and will continue to serve them as a judge . . . Politicians in Canada are notoriously corrupt . . . the average member of Parliament is a crook." This was tough talk in the 1920s.

The labour struggles of Cape Breton reopened in the summer of 1923 when the steelworkers at the Sydney steel mill went on strike in an attempt to win the right to bargain with BESCO. Masked strikers stopped maintenance workers from entering the plant. A magistrate, trying to read the Riot Act, was knocked unconscious. Canadian soldiers and an ill-trained provincial police force were sent to the scene. "One old woman over 70 years of age was beaten insensible and may die," McLachlan told miners. "A boy of nine years of age was trampled under the horses' feet and had his breastbone crushed in. One woman, beaten over the head with a police club, gave premature birth to a child. The child is dead and the woman's life is despaired of." There was only one answer: at the end of June, McLachlan led his men out on strike.

It was a laudable action, but it ignored the miners' own collective agreement with BESCO. The United Mineworkers had a powerful tradition of honouring its agreements to the letter— and demanding that employers do the same. The U.S. head office of the Union ordered the strike ended, McLachlan removed and Silby Barrett put back in charge. The coal miners reluctantly obeyed.

The steelworkers' strike collapsed. Wolvin then imposed a further 20 percent wage cut on the miners and, when they came out on strike, waited them out. Hundreds of miners and steel-workers were "blacklisted" so that they could never hope to find work in Cape Breton again. McLachlan was arrested, convicted of uttering "seditious remarks" during the 1923 strike, and sentenced to two years in jail. Nationwide protests soon won his freedom but the struggle grew only more bitter.

Poverty, hunger and illness grew in the mining communities of northern Cape Breton and on the Nova Scotia mainland. On March 2, 1925, BESCO stopped extending credit at its company

stores. That was no small matter to families dependent on the "pluck me," as the stores were known, when wages were low and work was scarce. Appeals to BESCO were fruitless. Wolvin finally declared that, since the stores were losing money, he would close them down.

On Friday, March 6, 1925, the miners heeded McLachlan's appeals from his new position as editor of the *Maritime Labor Herald:* a 100 percent strike. Every coal mine in Nova Scotia shut down as miners marched out. The miners' cause rallied unions and church organizations across Canada. It was not enough. As a Communist, McLachlan felt no qualms about approaching a Soviet delegation in Canada to purchase flour. On March 20, 1925, the All Russian Union of Miners cabled $5000 to their comrade, J.B. McLachlan. Cape Breton union leaders were badly split; they knew how the gift would be interpreted. The desperate miners had no such qualms; they voted to take the money.

The leaders were more far-sighted. BESCO management had no trouble proving to Canadians that the strike was part of an international Communist conspiracy. At New Waterford, a mining town, BESCO shut off the water supply because it passed through company pipes and also turned off the electricity. More

The Women's Labour League in Winnipeg, preparing relief supplies for the Cape Breton strikers in 1925. The miners' desperate struggle aroused considerable sympathy among churches and labour organizations across the country.

company police were sent to defend its property. Miners from the region responded by gathering in the town. Finally, the miners marched to the BESCO property in their hundreds. BESCO guards, on horseback, met the attack with a baton charge. In the melee, miners were hit by clubs and one miner, William Davis, died. Sheer numbers prevailed. Miners took over the power plant and pump house and marched off thirty guards and BESCO officials to the New Waterford jail.

Rioting spread. At night, miners with blackened faces broke into the company stores at Caledonia, New Waterford, New Aberdeen, Donkin, Dominion, Glace Bay and Passchendaele. In some cases, clerks had foreseen the break-ins and rearranged the goods to frustrate looters—shoes and boots were mixed up so they did not match in size or colour. One man lugged home a ninety-six pound sack filled with what he thought was flour. Next morning, when his mother who was almost blind, tried to make biscuits, she discovered that the booty was a bag of wall plaster.

The strike carried on into the summer, with the provincial government throwing its support behind Wolvin. "When those who are fomenting this trouble see fit to accept money from the Red Internationale and to parade under the Red Flag in preference to the British Flag, it is time the public took notice," stated Premier Ernest H. Armstrong.

The crisis eventually drew to a close. In the election of June 25, 1925, Armstrong's Liberal government was defeated, winning only three seats to the Conservatives' forty. The new premier, E.N. Rhodes, was elected on his promise to end the strike. A compromise was arranged. The miners would have a six-month contract with a 6 to 8 percent wage cut. All workers would be rehired. BESCO in return would receive one-fifth of its coal royalties back from the Nova Scotia government.

What was the price of the conflict? The cost of supporting the troops in Cape Breton was $325,000. The provincial government's total loss reached at least $550,000. The company lost $1,505,430 in profits. Wolvin lost his job. But the big losers were the miners themselves: they lost over $7 million dollars in wages and were forced to return to work with a salary decrease.

On November 11, 1925, Armistice Day, a royal commission began its hearings into the coal strike. A wide assortment of expert witnesses were called. Doctors testified that many infants had died from malnutrition because of the strike. Health inspectors detailed the mass outbreaks of scarlet fever, diptheria, smallpox, typhoid, tuberculosis and polio—outbreaks attributable to poor sewage disposal and inadequate company housing. The commission recommended that BESCO sell the company houses to the miners and improve sanitary conditions in company mining towns as soon as possible.

The most dramatic testimonies at the hearings were those of arch-rivals Wolvin and McLachlan. Wolvin maintained that a wage decrease was necessary because of depressed world markets and foreign competition. Then McLachlan presented to the commission the BESCO profit and loss balance sheets for the years 1922 to 1925. Where they came from he would not say. The figures suggested that BESCO had been making steady profits throughout the early twenties. There was no apparent reason for cutting wages.

The commission, however, ruled that the miners should take a wage cut, on the grounds that other miners around the world were taking cuts. The Cape Breton workers could not face another strike. However unjust the decision may have seemed, there was little they could do except take what small consolation they could in the fact that Roy Wolvin was fired by BESCO for his role in the strike.

So it ended. There was no victory.

REVIEW AND DISCUSSION

Key People and Ideas
Explain the importance of each of the following as they are discussed in the chapter.

J.S. Woodsworth	The Committee on Industrial and
R.B. Russell	International Relations
Ray Wolvin	The Canadian Brotherhood of
J.B. McLachlan	Railway Employees
Silby Barrett	The One Big Union
Ernest H. Armstrong	The Trades and Labour Congress
E.N. Rhodes	BESCO

Analysing the Issues
Answer each of the following questions, which deal with important issues raised in the chapter.

1. What were working conditions like in the twenties?
2. What political gains did labour make in the 1920s?
3. What effect did communism have on labour activity in the twenties?

Questions for Discussion
Think carefully about each of the following questions and discuss the issues which they raise.

1. Labour and management had very sharply divided views of the coal industry in Cape Breton. Which side, BESCO or the unions, do you think had the stronger case? Explain your reasons.
2. Did the miners and steelworkers gain much by their strikes in the 1920s? Were the strikes worth it?

6

THE ECONOMY: UP AND DOWN

After the wartime period of government controls on the economy, the Canadian business community in the 1920s was eager for things to return to what they regarded as normal—that is, to the free-enterprise system in which business operated with as little interference as possible from government. Their commitment to free enterprise was not, however, so strong that they could not make exceptions where it benefited them. A policy of high tariffs flagrantly contradicted the principles of free enterprise, but because it was necessary to their survival the central Canadian business elite supported it strongly. And, although they were philosophically opposed to publicly owned enterprise, the private sector supported state investment in cases where it was to their advantage, such as railways and, in a number of the provinces, hydro-electric power. Economic development in the 1920s generally meant that public policy and public investment served the interests of private, often foreign-owned, enterprise. Canada was pioneering its own peculiar blend of public and private ownership.

Although the 1920s are often regarded as a period of prosperity and optimism, it was not until the middle of the decade that the economy began to show particularly strong growth. In the early years of the decade, Canada was hit by recession. The gross national product declined sharply in 1921 and 1922. American tariff policy caused a drastic drop in the volume and value of Canadian exports. Farmers were particularly hard hit, and business failures and bankruptcies were also numerous between 1921 and 1923. Several banks came close to collapse, and one, the Home Bank, did fail.

All this meant considerable hardship for the working class, as wages fell and unemployment rose. But because both the business community and its political allies were in favour of free enterprise, the King government felt no need to do anything to strengthen the economy. Nor did it attempt to reduce the hardship of the farmers and workers and small businessmen who were the most severely hurt by the recession.

By the middle of the decade, the economy had begun to turn around. Between 1924 and 1929, there was a boom which transformed the Canadian economy. The most important factor was rapid expansion in the natural resource sector, particularly in energy, forestry and mining.

The Natural Resources Boom

Secure supplies of energy were essential to economic expansion, both in the resource and manufacturing sectors. The principal energy source developed in the 1920s was hydro-electric power. The decade began with the opening in December 1921 of the world's largest hydro-electric plant at Queenston, Ontario. The

Opposite page:
A lumberyard in Fort Frances in northwestern Ontario. Forestry was just one of the natural resource industries which fuelled Canada's economic boom in the mid-twenties. This yard was part of the largest mill in Fort Frances, owned by a group of lumber manufacturers from Minneapolis in the United States. Increasing American investment was an important trend in Canadian economic development in the twenties.

cost had been enormous not only because of the size of the project but because it had required a canal to be built around Niagara Falls to divert the Niagara River. The Queenston generating station was just the first in a series of projects undertaken in the twenties by the Ontario Hydro-Electric Power Commission under the aggressive direction of Sir Adam Beck. The same enthusiasm for expansion prevailed in other provinces as well. Overall, the output of electricity quadrupled between 1921 and 1930.

The power industry was partly owned by public and partly by private enterprise. In Ontario, the publicly owned utility became so powerful that it held an effective monopoly on the province's hydro-electric resources. Public ownership was also a factor in Manitoba and New Brunswick, whereas in Quebec the industry was in private hands. But whether they were privately or publicly owned, the power companies had a common goal: to supply cheap electricity to private industry. And whatever their ownership, the power companies saw no limit to their future growth; they assumed that the level of demand established in the twenties would continue indefinitely, and they planned their expansion accordingly. One enthusiastic journalist predicted that the industry would eventually employ six million new workers and raise the population to forty milion—an expectation that has not yet been met.

The boom in the pulp and paper industry was mainly due to increased production of newsprint. Ninety percent of Canada's newsprint was exported, 75 percent of it to the United States. The American newspaper trade expanded very quickly in the 1920s. There were more newspapers printed, and they had twice as many pages as they had had before 1920. With its abundant forest resources, Canada was able to expand its energy sources, transportation network and labour force very rapidly as the American demand for newsprint grew. In 1930, Canada's paper mills could produce three times the newsprint that they had been able to make in 1920. There were mills in six of Canada's nine provinces (Quebec, Ontario, British Columbia, New Brunswick, Nova Scotia and Manitoba), and the industry employed a large work force. Provincial governments in Ontario, Quebec, British Columbia and New Brunswick supported the industry by banning the export of unprocessed pulpwood cut on crown land; the newsprint had to be made in Canada—an instance of public policy tailored to private sector development. The governments were less vigorous in applying regulations to conserve and protect forest resources.

The same kind of rapid development occurred in the mining sector. The mineral wealth of the Canadian Shield made it a focus of economic activity throughout the decade. Although the

Bush Pilots
Most of the bush pilots of the twenties were ex-airmen from the First World War. Some had been barnstorming around the country putting on daring air shows at fairs. Others were looking for work and excitement. They found both during the mining boom of the late twenties, carrying gold bricks, live goats, dynamite and a motley assortment of prospectors, promoters, miners and entrepreneurs to and from remote northern mine sites. Often they flew without instruments, filtered their gas through their own felt hats and guessed their directions since much of the north was still uncharted.

reality of northern mining was anything but romantic, many Canadians were caught up in the excitement surrounding it and believed that the exploitation of the Shield's mineral resources would bring untold wealth to the country. New mining discoveries occurred almost monthly, drawing risk capital from both the business community and the general public.

The airplane which was a product of the war now became the workhorse of the north. Across the unnamed lakes of the Shield, these fragile machines, often flown by ex-wartime pilots, carried geologists, prospectors, diamond drillers and stock promoters in search of new mineral deposits. The new importance of airplanes led to the creation of a Canadian air service in 1920, renamed the Royal Canadian Air Force on April 1, 1924. During its early years, it spent much of its time carrying out civilian duties such as spraying forests and patrolling them for fire, monitoring coastal fishing and preventing smuggling, and performing emergency airlifts. The RCAF also did extensive aerial photography, which was an important part of opening up the north and determining its mining potential.

The results of all this exploration and investment were impressive. In provinces where the mining industry was already established, production increased and new mines were developed. Communities in Ontario such as Sudbury, with its huge deposits of nickel, and Kirkland Lake, with its gold mines, flourished in the twenties. The same was true of mining towns, such as Trail, in British Columbia.

New mining operations were set up in other provinces too. In Quebec, gold and copper reserves at Rouyn–Noranda began to be developed in the mid-twenties, and asbestos mining brought new economic life to the Eastern Townships. In Manitoba too there were major new developments. By 1927 the Hudson Bay Mining and Smelting Company Limited had been formed to develop copper and zinc deposits at Flin Flon. Eventually, development of Manitoba's mineral resources generated new business for the hitherto underused Hudson Bay Railway.

The exploration of the Canadian Shield was initially promp-

A bush plane on a mercy flight to deliver diptheria vaccine to Fort Vermilion in northern Alberta in January 1929 makes a stop for engine repairs at Peace River. Flying an open-cockpit plane in the middle of winter was extremely hazardous. Like so many bush pilots, the pilot of this flight, Wilfrid "Wop" May, had been a pilot during the First World War. In 1918 he narrowly escaped being shot down by von Richthofen, the "Red Baron." After the war, he became one of Canada's leading bush pilots.

ted by the search for precious metals, gold and silver. Between 1921 and 1929 there were great increases in the production of gold and silver. There were even greater increases in the output of base metals such as nickel, lead, zinc and copper. Base metals were particularly important in new industries such as automobile, electrical and radio manufacture, and new, more efficient processing techniques made it possible to supply these markets. Again, the main buyer was the United States, and again governments did everything they could to encourage mining developments. They built railways, roads and power plants to service the new mining communities and did little to regulate the companies' activities or tax their profits.

Transportation: Railways, Roads, Cars

While natural resources fuelled the Canadian economic boom of the late 1920s, advances in transportation probably transformed more lives. Railways reached the height of their power and technological excellence during the decade, partly because they were fighting a new competitor, the automobile. If Canada's railway age had created steel and heavy engineering industries in Sydney, Hamilton, Sault Ste. Marie, Montreal and Winnipeg, the automotive age generated a denser cluster of industries in southern Ontario. Electrical, rubber, petro-chemical and leather industries depended on auto factories as an outlet for their products.

A great and enormously costly restructuring of the Canadian railway system had culminated in 1919 with the takeover of the Grand Trunk and its Pacific extension to Prince Rupert. Arbitrators agreed that the shares in the old railway were worthless. The real issue was whether the Grand Trunk and the other bankrupt railways would be handed over to the Canadian Pacific Railway to run as a giant monopoly or whether the government could be trusted to run a system in competition with the CPR.

Under a new American-born manager, Sir Henry Thornton, Meighen's creation, the Canadian National Railways, appeared to flourish. Thornton, well aware of the problems in his sprawling railway empire, decided that the best way to succeed was to be bold. The Canadian National became a transportation giant, with beautiful white liners serving the West Indies, magnificent hotels to attract tourists, even a national radio system to entertain passengers on the CNR's trains. Sir Edward Beatty, Thornton's rival at the head of the CPR, matched him in energy and imagination. Never, before or since, was it more comfortable or convenient to travel by rail.

Yet the railways were not really competing against each other but against a far more deadly enemy, the convenience of the automobile. The magnificent facilities and service of the CPR and the CNR were no answer to the flexibility and convenience of

Opposite page: Dining in comfort on the Canadian Pacific Railway. The intense competition between the CPR and the CNR meant that each railway tried to outdo the other in providing luxury service and accommodation in their hotels and aboard their trains and ocean liners.

the private car. In Ontario, Sir Adam Beck had planned a system of "radial railways," powered by surplus electricity from the Ontario Hydro-Electric Power Commission, emerging like the spokes of a wheel to provide cheap access to the cities. What was the point of such a system, asked Ernest Drury, when farmers had cars and roads?

Today, it is hard to imagine how both city and country dwellers were once dependent on horses. The transformation happened in the 1920s. For many years, horses continued to haul milk wagons, bread carts and a little freight from railway stations and factories but cars and trucks took their place in increasing numbers. Automobiles in the 1920s would now seem almost impossibly unreliable and difficult to drive. A journey of 150 kilometres was ambitious. Fifteen kilometres an hour was a common speed limit in cities or towns. Headlights, brakes and clutches were all undependable and any driver expected frequent stops to change a flat tire. Roads were twisting, single-lane, tree-lined gravel ribbons in most of Canada. On the prairies, roads were straight but a rain storm turned them into rivers of mud that could swallow a car up to its hubs and running boards.

Despite these problems, automobiles became immensely popular. Owning a car liberated a farm family and extended the range of towns it could visit for shopping and socializing. For young people, a car meant freedom from supervision. To the adventurous, it was a chance to explore the countryside or the city. The automobile was the key to owning a summer cottage away from the well-established resorts.

In turn, the automobile fed a host of spin-off industries. By 1929, 13 000 workers in Canada—most of them in Ontario—were directly employed in the auto industry and many thousands more were employed in related activities, from highway building to operating service stations. The petroleum business expanded to provide gasoline, grease and oil. The growing market for petroleum products led to a growth in exploration. New fields were developed in Texas and Oklahoma, in Mexico, South America, Russia and the Middle East. In Alberta, the search for oil led to discoveries in the Turner Valley near Calgary.

The rubber industry expanded to satisfy the demand for tires. A boom in road construction began in the 1920s and has hardly abated. Tar, gravel and cement were in demand as governments began to develop all-weather highway surfaces, particularly on roads which would attract tourists from the United States. British Columbia, which had followed the British example by driving on the left side of the road, switched sides in 1923 to avoid confusing American visitors.

Railways complained of the competition for passengers but they were sublimely confident that they would move the nation's

Opposite page:
One of the first oil rigs in the Turner Valley near Calgary. By the mid-twenties, the car industry had created a huge market for oil and gas, and investors and promoters were rushing to take advantage of the boom.

A tire shop in Winnipeg, 1921. As a result of the car boom, the tire business flourished in the twenties. Tires were notoriously unreliable. It was quite possible to have as many as ten flat tires on a 200-kilometre journey, so motorists had to be adept at patching inner tubes by the side of the road. Balloon tires—fatter tires which ran at lower air inflation—were developed in the twenties, and they made for greater durability and a more comfortable ride.

freight. They were wrong. W.F. Maclean, a Conservative MP and former newspaper owner, warned in 1926 that:

> . . . the automobile constitutes a menace to our railways. I refer to the competition of the automobile and the motor truck on our new highways in Ontario, Quebec and other provinces. The automobiles and motor trucks are securing nearly all of the local traffic by which the railways have so far been sustained, and where that competition is going to end I am at a loss to know.

A Progressive, G.G. Coote, was more of an optimist. His answer, true to form, was to foster the automobile in Canada by free trade:

> The greatest improvement in transportation facilities since the invention of the steam locomotive is the automobile, both freight and passenger . . . The greatest competitor that Canada has today is the United States. The United States has motor trucks available to her population at two-thirds the price at which they can be purchased by the people in Canada. The United States has one motor car for every six of her population, while Canada has one to every fourteen of her population.

Although the air age had begun, neither car nor train had much to fear in the 1920s from the airplane. The wartime aircraft factory at Toronto was closed by early 1919, never to open again. By the end of the decade, a small, unprofitable service took passengers from Toronto to Buffalo. But along the populated southern strip, railways and roads would continue to handle almost all transportation needs for many years to come.

However, this was the decade when the Canadian north was opened. It could not have happened without tough, intrepid bush pilots, willing to push their fragile aircraft into extremes of weather and terrain. In the air, the spirit of adventure found a new dimension.

The Americanization of the Canadian Economy

Because of a 35 percent tariff on cars imported into Canada, it was to the advantage of American auto manufacturers to establish branch plants. If the cars were made in Canada, they could be sold without a surcharge in Canada and exported tariff-free to other parts of the British Empire. Ownership of the Canadian auto industry became more and more concentrated in fewer hands, and by the end of the decade these hands were all American. By 1930, three-quarters of all the cars made in Canada were produced by the three big American car manufacturers, Ford, General Motors and Chrysler.

The Americanization of the Canadian auto industry points to a fundamental structural change underlying much of the economic activity in Canada in the 1920s. For business to thrive, it needed investment capital. Canada had always depended on foreign investment, and the principal source had been Britain. Weakened by the First World War, Britain was by 1920 investing little new capital in Canada. The United States stepped into its place, eager to develop Canada's raw materials and extend the market for American manufactured goods.

Led by Quebec, political and business leaders in Canada looked to the United States for the money to finance mines, pulp and paper mills, power installations and industrial plants. By 1922 the United States had taken over from Britain as Canada's biggest source of foreign investment. American investment totalled 50 percent of the foreign investment in Canada. By the end of the decade, it had reached 60 percent—$4 billion.

But there was a crucial difference between British and American investment in the Canadian economy. Most British investment was in the form of loans; Canadians went into debt but they retained ownership of their resources and enterprises. By contrast most American investment in Canada was direct: rather than lending money, American investors bought into Canada. They took direct control, often outright ownership, of factories and mines and mills. The pattern of branch-plant development in the auto industry was duplicated in other sectors. By 1930 a third of the pulp and paper industry was controlled by Americans. Forty percent of the mining industry was also under American control. Hudson Bay Mining and Smelting which owned the mines at Flin Flon was backed by the H.P. Whitney Company of New York. Noranda Mines also had considerable American investment.

While this massive wave of investment from the United States helped to fuel Canada's boom in the twenties, there were also some disadvantages which became more apparent as time went on. Most Americans investing in Canada were after raw materials which they then took to the United States for processing and manufacturing. Canadian governments implemented some protective legislation in cases such as newsprint and automobiles. But these were exceptions rather than the rule. Quebec's experience with asbestos was far more typical. In an attempt to force the Americans to remove their 25 percent tariff on imports of goods manufactured from asbestos, the Quebec government threatened to ban exports of unprocessed asbestos. The American-based mining companies responded by threatening to supply themselves from Rhodesia (now Zimbabwe). The provincial government had little choice but to back off.

The overall effect of this pattern in the economy as a whole was that secondary, manufacturing industries did not develop quickly in Canada. This limited both the number and the type of jobs open to Canadians. As a result, almost a million Canadians emigrated to the United States between 1921 and 1931. The emigrants included both unskilled workers and highly trained specialists.

As long as times were prosperous, there seemed little reason to analyze the effects of American control or speculate about the vulnerability of a resource-based economy or worry about the long-term effects of such rapid economic growth. There seemed to be no limit to Canada's prosperity. The stock markets, the Grain Exchange and intense corporate competition all fuelled the heady speculation among Canadian business interests. These speculative ventures were almost totally free of government regulations. Investors took greater and greater risks, tempted by the chance of making a huge fortune. Very few people felt, as did financier Sir Joseph Flavelle, that the investment community was displaying an "almost irrational faith" in Canada's future.

The Rise and Fall of Sir Henry Pellatt
It is easier to understand the business climate of the 1920s if we understand the businessmen of the time. One of the most flamboyant wheeler-dealers of the decade was Sir Henry Pellatt.

Pellatt was the son of a stockbroker. Prior to the First World

War, he made a fortune through investments in electrical utilities. He made large amounts of money by forming companies, marketing their shares and then selling the companies. By the close of the nineteenth century, Pellatt's Toronto Electric Light Company was able to light the streets of the city and power the streetcars. When he sold his interests, he became an even richer man and reinvested his wealth in western land.

Knighted for his financial achievements in 1905, Sir Henry Pellatt needed a dwelling suitable to his aristocratic title. What better accommodation than a castle? He chose a four-hectare site in Toronto, with an eye to making profits from the land development that would follow the construction of his castle. It took four years to build Casa Loma. Completed in 1914, the magnificent structure was an unmatched expression of Sir Henry's extravagance. The castle had thirty bathrooms, twenty-five fireplaces and ninety-eight rooms. It was lit with 5000 lightbulbs.

Sir Henry Pellatt's displays of wealth were enough to convince one of his main creditors, the Home Bank, to extend him unlimited credit to finance his ventures. By 1921, however, the bank had received a worrisome report on Sir Henry's financial empire. The report stated that "there is no outlook for it but bankruptcy" if Pellatt continued on his free-spending course. The Home Bank had extended credit to Sir Henry on the basis of

A busy free auto laundry in the Humber River, Toronto.

By the end of the twenties, Casa Loma was becoming derelict. Finally, in the 1930s, the city decided to demolish it. At the last moment, the Kiwanis Club took over the castle and restored it. Today Casa Loma is one of Toronto's major tourist attractions.

his own estimates of the value of his land holdings around Casa Loma. Whereas he had valued one piece of property at over $700,000, the investigator's report put its real value at less than $150,000. Obviously both Pellatt and the Home Bank were in trouble.

Although it was relatively small, the Home Bank was an important financial institution, with seventy branches across Canada and some 60 000 depositors, most of whom were ordinary Canadians. The bank tried desperately to hide the truth. Money deposited was used to pay dividends and interest, but there was little capital to back up the bank. On April 20, 1923, another report stated that Pellatt's affairs were "in a mess." Could the Home Bank recover its loans?

There was no escape. On August 17, 1923, the Home Bank declared bankruptcy with outstanding debts of $18,486,978. Nearly $2 million of this debt was money lent to Sir Henry Pellatt, money which could not be recovered. The Home Bank's failure shook the complacency of many middle-class Canadians who had invested in the bank itself or in Pellatt's enterprises. Life savings were wiped out overnight. The damage was particularly severe on the prairies because many of the Home Bank's shareholders and depositors were westerners. In 1924, several Home Bank officials were arrested, charged with falsifying records and convicted.

The shock of the Home Bank failure triggered the rapid collapse of the Pellatt empire. Lady Pellatt died of a heart attack in 1924. The problems involved in running the castle were draining Sir Henry as well; his servants alone cost $40,000 a year, his coal bill $15,000 and his taxes $12,000. Shortly after the death of his wife, Sir Henry gave Casa Loma to the city of Toronto.

Then the auctions began. For several days, Sir Henry's prized possessions—suits of armour, antique furniture, books, paintings—were auctioned off to bidders from across North America. One and a half million dollars worth of furnishings were sold for $250,000. When Sir Henry Pellatt died in 1939, he was living with his former chauffeur in a small house in Mimico near Toronto. His assets totalled $185.

The failure of Sir Henry Pellatt was a shock, and the collapse of the Home Bank was one of the events that eventually initiated some regulation of banking in Canada. But at the time it was not considered an indicator of things to come. There were still many Canadians with boundless enthusiasm, ready to seize opportunities to open the north, to gamble for great rewards on the stock market, to invest in the new wonders of the age: the car, the airplane, the radio and all the other spin-off industries that these generated. It was not until 1929 that Canadians realized just how unrealistic their hopes for continued prosperity were.

The Crash and the Depression

Such was the optimism generated by the boom years of the 1920s that very few Canadians were prepared for the crash of 1929 and the Depression of the 1930s. Despite disturbing signs of instability in the international economy, the stock market in New York rose well into 1929. With the economies of the two countries now so closely linked, Canadian stock exchanges in Montreal and Toronto followed suit. And they did so too when the New York exchange began to fall in September and crashed in October. Companies such as International Nickel, Noranda Mines and the Ford Motor Company—key players in Canada's prosperity in the twenties—were among those most badly hurt.

The stock market crash was just one aspect of the economic collapse. There were other, deeper causes of the Depression in Canada, some of them internal and some of them having to do with the international economy. Canada's resource-based economy was extremely dependent on export trade; 80 percent of Canada's agricultural, forestry and mining output went to foreign buyers. As early as the summer of 1929, there were ominous signs. Wheat prices were declining, a problem made even more serious by the enormous crops of 1928 and the stiff competition from other wheat-producing nations—the United States, Argentina, Australia and the Soviet Union. Good crops in Italy, Germany, France and even Britain in 1929 made the situation worse.

By the early 1930s the price of wheat had hit rock bottom, and the effect on the economy was catastrophic.

Other sectors of the economy were similarly hard hit. Every economic indicator in the United States pointed to trouble, and that meant trouble for Canada as well. The American market for newsprint was becoming weaker and weaker. By 1927 Canadian production of newsprint had begun to exceed the American demand for it. The immediate result was intense competition; control of the industry became concentrated in the hands of a very few companies, as smaller and weaker firms were taken over or driven under. After 1930 the imbalance between supply and demand became so disastrous that mills were closed or went bankrupt, and employment fell drastically. The huge investment made in the 1920s became a huge liability in the 1930s.

Soon the prices and quantity of exports of metals, minerals, lumber, pulp and paper, and fish also began to fall sharply. The railways were badly hurt by the collapse of freight and tourist traffic. Railway hotels and stations were left unfinished in Montreal and Vancouver. Orders for new equipment were cancelled, and that in turn hurt the steel industry. Other manufacturing interests were also hurt, particularly the farm implement and auto makers. Canadian farmers had purchased 17 000 tractors in 1928; in 1932, with their purchasing power wiped out by the collapse of wheat prices, they bought only 892. Finally, with the collapse of both the manufacturing and resource sectors, the power industry was left with huge surpluses of electricity. The boom was clearly over.

The twenties had been years of great hope but, as the crash and the Depression proved, the reality had been rather different. The boom had made a few people very rich, but it had not put enough money in the hands of enough people to sustain the market for such vastly increased production. Productivity had increased enormously but wages had not. The gap between the rich and the poor widened steadily. In 1929, most workers in Canada were making less than $1000—not enough, according to the Department of Labour, for a family to keep up a "minimum standard of decency." Nor was wealth distributed across the country; neither the prairie provinces nor the Maritimes benefited nearly as much as the rest of the country from the prosperity of the twenties. Trade was brisk, but it was trade that went north-south, between Canada and the U.S., not east-west across the country. By the end of the decade, the real economic situation was becoming all too apparent. The mass unemployment, farm bankruptcies and business failures of the 1930s lay ahead, threatening far greater hardship and deprivation for most Canadians.

REVIEW AND DISCUSSION

Key People and Ideas
Explain the importance of each of the following as they are discussed in the chapter.

Sir Adam Beck   Pulp and paper
Sir Henry Thornton   The Canadian Shield
Sir Henry Pellatt   The Royal Canadian Air Force
                       Asbestos
                       The Canadian National Railways
                       The automobile
                       American investment
                       The Home Bank
                       The stock market crash

Analysing the Issues
Answer each of the following questions, which deal with important issues raised in the chapter.

1. What was the role of private enterprise in the 1920s?
2. Why was the Canadian Shield so important at this particular time?
3. What effect did the automobile have on both the Canadian economy and on everyday life?

Questions for Discussion
Think carefully about each of the following questions and discuss the issues which they raise.

1. The natural resources sector of the Canadian economy expanded rapidly in the 1920s. What were the advantages and disadvantages of Canada's dependence on natural resource industries? What are the consequences today?
2. American investment in Canada increased enormously in the 1920s. Do you think that this was beneficial to Canada? What effect does American investment have on the country now?

7

CULTURE AND ENTERTAINMENT: HIGHBROW AND LOWBROW

There was a freshness and a brashness about Canadian culture in the twenties. For English-speaking Canadians at least, the feeling that they were second-rate colonials had begun to disappear in the trenches of the First World War. With growing self-confidence, Canadian writers, painters and radio dramatists devoted their energies to interpreting the Canadian identity. This new cultural nationalism was not simply a reaction against older cultural attitudes. It was also a response to a new challenge. Just as American involvement in the Canadian economy increased rapidly in the 1920s, so too did its influence on Canadian culture.

The most dramatic expression of cultural nationalism in the 1920s was the art of the Group of Seven, a loosely organized association of painters based in Toronto. The original members of the Group were James E.H. MacDonald, Lawren Harris, A.Y. Jackson, Fred Varley, Frank Carmichael, Arthur Lismer and Frank Johnston. Later, in the mid-twenties, Johnston dropped out and A.J. Casson took his place. In the early thirties, Edwin Holgate of Montreal and LeMoine FitzGerald of Winnipeg joined the Group.

The original Group began to work together before the First World War because of their shared interest in painting a new subject: the landscape of the Canadian Shield. In their early years, they worked alongside another painter, Tom Thomson, who died mysteriously in 1917 while canoeing in Algonquin Park in Ontario. Thomson's most famous painting, *The Jack Pine,* is representative in spirit and style of the Group's early period.

The Group made its official entry into the Canadian art world when it held an exhibition in Toronto in May 1920. The Group's paintings were aggressive, bold, sometimes stark, sometimes cluttered, and always in celebration of nature—Canadian nature. It was impressionistic art that glorified the raw, untamed wilderness of Canada's north.

The Group's choice of subject was a radical departure for the Canadian art world, where tastes and attitudes had largely been formed by European subjects, styles, painters and critics. Canadian collectors were much more accustomed to buying traditional European art, such as Dutch landscapes, than any kind of Canadian art—let alone the wild canvases of the Group of Seven. Commenting on the effect of that first exhibition, A.Y. Jackson said, ''Canadians were challenged to replace the Dutch cow with the northern bull moose.''

Some members of the artistic community were not favourably impressed by the Group's work. As early as 1913, one hostile critic referred to the Group's style of painting as the ''Hot Mush School.'' In 1916 another critic described their techniques as a ''rigid formula for ugliness.''

Public and critical recognition did slowly come. As the twen-

If the walls of the Canadian section of the British Empire Exhibition are to be covered with crude cartoons of the Canadian Wilds, devoid of perspective, atmospheric feeling and sense of texture, it is going to be a bad advertisement for this country. We should advise the Department of Immigration and Colonization to intervene to prevent such a catastrophe.

Saturday Night
September 15, 1923

Opposite page:
Outside a movie theatre in Toronto in 1923. Movies—especially Hollywood movies—became enormously popular in the 1920s.

Barns, La Malbaie, Quebec, painted by A.Y. Jackson in 1926. A leading member of the Group of Seven, Jackson was committed to the development of a landscape style that would faithfully represent Canada. He painted across the country, but he was particularly drawn to the rural areas of his native Quebec.

ties went on, the Group conquered much of both the public and the art world. It is ironic that these most Canadian of painters owed some of that triumph to the praise they received from British reviewers after a successful exhibition in London in 1924. The Group was supported by the National Gallery of Canada throughout the twenties and found wealthy patrons to pay for their travel to the north they painted so devotedly. When the Group broke up in the early thirties, its work had won widespread public and critical recognition. The bull moose had clearly won out over the Dutch cow.

The Group of Seven were not the only Canadian painters active in the twenties. Others, such as David Milne, pursued a line of development quite different from the nationalist emphasis of the Group of Seven. Milne's technical experimentation was important to later Canadian painters. Other artists had more in common with the Group. Of these perhaps the most notable was Emily Carr. After spending some years in the United States, England and France, Carr returned to her native British Columbia. In 1927 she travelled to eastern Canada and met members of the Group of Seven. Both their paintings and their encouragement, especially that of Lawren Harris, gave her renewed energy for her own art. She is particularly noted for the powerful and dramatic paintings of Indian villages and the brooding landscapes which she produced in this later period of her career.

Books, Magazines and Newspapers

Much of the literature written in the twenties did not make such a radical break with the past, nor did it demonstrate more than a shallow nationalism. Many established writers, such as Lucy Maud Montgomery, Stephen Leacock, Robert Service, Ralph Connor, Bliss Carman and Charles G.D. Roberts, continued to be popular. Newer fiction, both novels and short stories, tended to be lightweight—adventure stories and historical or sentimental romances, sometimes with a Canadian setting but never a very realistic one. Among the most successful of these were Mazo de la Roche's *Jalna* novels, the first of which was published in 1927.

There were some signs of a new direction in Canadian literature. A number of writers chose their subjects from everyday Canadian life and attempted to present them realistically. Books such as the novels of Frederick Philip Grove, Robert Stead's *Grain* (1926), Martha Ostenso's *Wild Geese* (1925) and Morley Callaghan's *Strange Fugitive* (1928) are all examples of this

Six of the seven members of the Group of Seven at the Arts and Letters Club in Toronto in 1921. From left to right, Fred Varley, A.Y. Jackson, Lawren Harris, Barker Fairley (art critic and promoter of the Group), F.H. Johnston, Arthur Lismer and J.E.H. MacDonald.

newer, more ambitious fiction. At the time, these novels were usually either denounced as immoral or dismissed as dull. But they did represent the beginnings of a modern Canadian literature.

The same split between the old and the new was evident in Canadian poetry in the twenties. Many of the poets produced little more than inferior imitations of the work of the previous generation of Canadian poets, Bliss Carman, Charles G.D. Roberts and Duncan Campbell Scott. They chose old-fashioned, conventional subjects and wrote about them in old-fashioned, conventional language.

But among some of the younger poets there was evidence of a new, modern Canadian poetry emerging. These poets experimented with new forms, new language and new subjects. Among them were Raymond Knister, E.J. Pratt, A.J.M. Smith and F.R. Scott. Although these new poets despised the sentimental nationalism—what Pratt described as the "Maple Leaf psychosis"—of the older generation of poets, they were nonetheless anxious to create a distinctively Canadian modern poetry. They were open to new influences from Europe and the United States, but they wanted to apply these techniques to contemporary Canadian experience.

Just as the Group of Seven chose the Canadian landscape as the subject of its art, many of these new novelists and poets were determined to capture in their work a Canadian sense of place, whether that place was the wilderness, the prairie, the city or the sea. Grove, Stead and others attempted to communicate the influence of a northern climate and landscape on the Canadian mentality. As Grove wrote in *The Turn of the Year* (1923), "Nobody, I believe, who lives farther south, where winter is a mere incident, can understand how we, at these outposts, feel the summer, that short, ardent orgy of life . . . ." Grove and Stead both wrote about the west and often depicted lonely figures, struggling with plough and harrow to master the prairie landscape. Grove recalled such a figure in his semi-autobiographical book, *In Search of Myself* (1946):

> Somewhere towards the end of my outward drive to town, I saw a man; and what is more, he was ploughing straight over the crest of a hill to the west, coming, when I caught sight of him, towards my trail. The town which I was approaching lay on the railway, in the dry belt of the country; the general verdict was that the surrounding district was unfit for farming. The mere fact, therefore, that this man was ploughing as he came over the crest of the hill was sufficiently arresting and even startling. Besides, outlined as he

Jalna, *the first of Mazo de la Roche's series of novels about an Ontario family, the Whiteoaks, and their home,* Jalna, *won the* Atlantic Monthly's *$10,000 award for the best novel of the year in 1927.*

The American novelist, Ernest Hemingway (centre), and his family in Toronto around 1923. Hemingway worked for several years for the *Toronto Star* both in Toronto—a city he loathed—and as a correspondent in Europe.

was against a tilted and spoked sunset in the western sky, he looked like a giant. Never before had I seen, between farm and town, a human being in all my drives.

Stead's poetry drew similar, sometimes heroic or nostalgic images of the prairie. In "The Homesteader," he created an image of the human being ennobled by the limitless prairie:

> For here, on the edge of creation,
> Lies, far as the vision can fling,
> A kingdom that's fit for a nation—
> A kingdom—and I am the king!

Such depictions may seem stereotyped today, but they were images of striking reality to many Canadian readers in the twenties. Often these images appealed even to city people, temporarily escaping to the countryside on gravel roads in new automobiles.

Writers in other parts of the country were also attempting to capture their own sense of place, whether it was Callaghan writing about Toronto or E.J. Pratt looking back from the same city to the harsh coast of his native Newfoundland. The cold, clinical, almost frightening language of Pratt's poetry exemplified the new modernism in Canadian literature.

Canadian literature of the twenties had its detractors. One critic, Douglas Bush, asserted in 1926 that "the salvation of Canadian literature would be a nationwide attack of writer's cramp lasting at least a decade . . . . Canadian writers simply do not know enough." Another critic, writing in *Canadian Forum* in 1928, doubted whether Canadian readers had a sophisticated understanding of books by Canadian authors:

> Most of our people are so actively engaged in tilling the soil or scrambling to the top of the tree in the industrial and commercial world that they have neither the time nor the inclination for reading poetry on the back porch . . . . If you write of the far north and the wild west and the picturesque east, seasoning well with allusions to the Canada goose, fir trees, maple leaves, snowshoes, northern lights, etc., the public grasp the fact that you are a Canadian poet, whose works are to be bought from the same patriotic motive that prompts the purchaser of Eddy's matches or a Massey Harris farm implement, and read along with Ralph Connor and Eaton's catalogue.

Even negative reactions such as these reflect the new interest in the state of Canadian culture. It had become a topic to be debated and discussed and analysed, and in the process it was beginning to establish its own distinctive voice. *Canadian Forum* itself was very much part of this process. Founded in 1920, it was a monthly magazine concerned with public affairs and the arts, and it quickly became the cutting edge of this new Canadian awareness. "Too often our convictions were borrowed from London, Paris or New York," wrote the *Forum* staff as they proceeded to publish new and thought-provoking Canadian poets, artists and writers. Two new academic journals, the *Dalhousie Review* and the *Canadian Historical Review,* also encouraged the new interest in Canadian culture. Taking this enthusiasm to an extreme, the *Canadian Bookman,* a monthly started up in 1919, praised anything and everything written in Canada, with little concern for its real merit.

Publishing companies too both benefited from and encouraged this lively cultural atmosphere. Firms such as Ryerson, McClelland and Stewart, Macmillan of Canada and Graphic Publishers published both new Canadian titles and reprints of earlier Canadian authors such as Susanna Moodie, T.C. Haliburton and Bliss Carman. Rapidly increasing university enrolment created an environment and a growing audience for all this new cultural activity.

More popular Canadian magazines also did well in the twenties. *Maclean's* was so successful that its owner, Col. John B. Maclean, was able to add to his list *Canadian Homes and Gardens* in 1925, *Mayfair* in 1927 and *Chatelaine* in 1928. There was, however, stiff competition from a whole range of American publications such as *Ladies Home Journal, Saturday Evening Post* and *McCall's.* The *Saturday Evening Post* could honestly claim to be "Canada's leading magazine;" its circulation in Canada was larger than that of *Maclean's,* the best-selling domestic publication. The Magazine Publishers' Association, which was established in 1922, campaigned through much of the decade for tax breaks and tariff protection against their American competitors. They particularly focused their attack on the "pulps," lurid fiction magazines with titles such as *Black Mask, Dime Detective* and *Spicy Adventure.* These, the MPA could argue, were damaging to Canada both morally and economically. The Canadian magazine industry won some limited protection in 1928, and these measures were strengthened in the early thirties.

The American influence was also felt in Canadian newspapers. Although the papers were Canadian-owned, they were increasingly dependent on American sources of information and entertainment. The growing importance of wire services, which

Don Wright (at the piano) and his jazz band in Winnipeg in 1922. Jazz—improvised music which combines African, European and American influences— became very popular in the 1920s.

used teletype machines to relay news to subscribing newspapers, meant that much of the international news printed in Canada came from American sources. Two of the three services available in Canada were American, Associated Press and United Press. The third, Canadian Press, provided Canadian news to its subscribers but relied on Associated Press for world news. To a considerable extent, Canadians saw the world beyond their borders through American eyes.

The Americanization of Canadian papers was also evident in the type of amusements they offered. American syndicates supplied Canadian papers with features ranging from personal advice columns to comics. The comics—black and white strips on weekdays, a colour section on Saturday—were especially popular. In 1923 the Toronto *Star Weekly* claimed it had doubled its sales when it started running a number of American comics, including *Bringing Up Father*, *Barney Google* and *Mutt and Jeff*.

Prohibition, Country Fairs and Chautauquas

Culture includes all the tastes, customs and pastimes of people. The debates over literature and art during the twenties involved a relatively small group of Canadians. There were other, more widely popular forms of entertainment, some old and some new.

Prohibition

There was one cultural issue which concerned almost all Canadians: prohibition. Was alcohol to be part of their social life or not? Was drinking the sign of cultural sophistication or cultural degeneration?

Most Canadians had supported the laws prohibiting the manufacture, importation and sale of liquor during the war—prohibition had been part of the war effort. Advocates of prohibition had seen it as a means both to conserve grain and to guarantee the sobriety of munitions workers.

After the war, there was sharp debate between prohibitionists and anti-prohibitionists. The Women's Christian Temperance Union (WCTU) collected statistical evidence that showed how Canadian society was improved by prohibition. Crimes and family violence, such as child and wife beating, dropped sharply when alcohol was unavailable. "Booze is no friend of the worker," echoed John Queen to workers in the mining town of Cobalt, Ontario. Some social commentators attributed the relative non-violence and orderliness of strikes in the twenties to the absence of alcohol.

Opponents of prohibition saw it both as an unjustifiable limitation on individual liberty and as an invitation to criminal activity. Bootlegging and rum-running became sources of profit for unscrupulous entrepreneurs. The potential for profit in smug-

gling liquor to the United States, where prohibition was retained until 1933, was even greater. Canadian fishing schooners were lured into rum-running. A rum-runner could earn $250 a month, plus a bonus of $100 for every load safely landed—much better than $30 a month fishing. The temptation was hard to resist.

Canadians in border towns and cities were also drawn into the illegal liquor trade. At night, armed convoys of powerful Buicks and Pierce-Arrows criss-crossed the border with loads of liquor. Gangland violence occured. American government officials were enraged at Canadian smuggling activities. Wealthy family businesses, such as that of the Bronfmans of Prince Albert, Saskatchewan, profited enormously from the lucrative liquor trade and later grew into huge distilling empires.

The effects of prohibition were also evident in other aspects of Canadian life. "Blind pigs" were places where liquor could be bought illegally during prohibition. Bootleggers survived the end of prohibition in Canada for the convenience of those who were barred from government liquor stores or who found the hours inconvenient.

By the end of the decade, the anti-liquor crusade was a thing of the past for most Canadians. Quebec abandoned prohibition in 1919, and support for it in other provinces declined steadily. In referenda, British Columbia voted against prohibition in 1920, Manitoba and Alberta in 1923 and Saskatchewan in 1924. In

The townspeople of Elk Lake, Ontario, look on as government agents dump 160 kegs of homebrew, taken in a raid on a "blind pig" (illegal bar), into the lake.

1927 Ontario gave up the cause by passing the Liquor Control Act, which legalized the sale of liquor through government stores. New Brunswick rejected prohibition in the same year, and Nova Scotia in 1930. Most provinces opted for a state monopoly on liquor sales, thereby creating an immense new source of revenue for their governments. By 1930, only Prince Edward Island retained prohibition.

Country Fairs

In hundreds of towns across Canada, the annual fair was the main social and cultural event of the year. The 22nd Annual Agricultural Fair held in 1920 in the booming Alberta town of Wetaskiwin was just such an event. A baseball tournament was held the first day, with a $100 prize for the top team. A brass band provided background music while local players showed off their best Babe Ruth imitations. There were horse races of varying types and quality. Sometimes the animals were harnessed to sulkies, light two-wheeled carriages for one person. Other times, semi-professional riders raced the horses. On occasion, local boys raced for $35 prizes. Altogether, $370 was available in prize money—a large sum for those days.

The brass band played with particular enthusiasm for the automobile races. Special racing cars tried to beat the 43.2-second record for the half-mile track. These races drew the biggest crowds.

A.G. Boucher's Big United Shows provided high wire gymnasts. A midway boasted a merry-go-round, a ferris wheel, circus organs, fast-cooked foods and games of chance. In the grandstand ring amateur cowhands rode bucking horses and roped frightened heifers. "Keep a-Smiling" advertised the Driard Hotel whose proprietor, C. Smith, always smiled on fair days because business was so brisk. The local ice cream parlour did a steady business too.

Chautauqua

Chautauqua? The name is almost meaningless today, but in the twenties Chautauqua was the most exciting experience in the way of live entertainment for many small-town Canadians. Taking its name from the lake in New York State where it began, Chautauqua was a travelling assembly of musicians, actors, singers, lecturers and puppeteers. It offered a mix of education and entertainment. In its early years in the 1870s, it was associated with Methodism and temperance. By the 1920s, it had lost most of its religious emphasis.

John M. Erickson and his wife, Nola, set up a Canadian network, Dominion Chautauquas, in Alberta in 1917; after 1926 it was called Canadian Chautauquas. Their shows travelled extensively, especially in the west.

When the Chautauqua came to town, a large tent was erected and for four to six days the whole community was entertained. A different performance was presented each day. Then the tent was folded and the assembly proceeded to the next town to do the whole series of shows over again.

Radio, Sports and Movies

In the 1920s country fairs and Chautauquas faced an immense challenge from new forms of entertainment. By 1930 the popularity of radio, professional sports and movies had transformed Canadian cultural life.

Radio

Cars, trucks, roads and airplanes all brought Canadians closer together in the twenties by reducing the time it took to travel the vast distances in this country. Another new technology had a similar effect on the cultural life of the nation: radio provided instant communication without travel. The radio craze was one of the main features of culture in the twenties. Young and old marvelled at how the human voice could be transmitted through the air in the form of radio waves and be received by simple crystal sets.

The first radio programs in Canada were broadcast from Montreal in 1920, and the public appetite for radio soon proved to be enormous. By 1923 Canadians had bought just under 10 000 radios; the number had risen to 297 000 by 1929. New radio stations began to pop up all over the country. Although a licence to broadcast was required under legislation passed in 1913, some Canadians simply got a transmitter and went on the airwaves without a licence.

Licensed or not, radio stations broadcast just about anything that could be put through the transmitter. Bands assembled and played live for audiences in remote corners of Canada. Untrained, unpaid, unknown radio enthusiasts became famous overnight as their voices entered lonely farmhouses in Saskatchewan and bustling tenements in Montreal.

The reason for this widespread use of amateur local talent by Canadian radio stations was summed up by one broadcaster:

> We had a hard time in Canada trying to compete with the programs the Americans had on NBC and CBS. We had so little money . . . . The only way to compete was to exploit local talent. Our best singers and instrumentalists performed for small fees or no fee at all . . . . We also did programs by local choral societies and we had spelling bees and debates between local schools. Events of that nature made radio a part of family life.

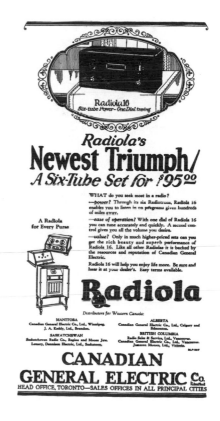

Canada's first nationwide radio network was operated by the CNR. When Sir Henry Thornton took over the railway in 1922, he decided that it should have a radio broadcasting department. The result was a cross-Canada radio broadcasting network. In 1929, Austin Weir, the head of the CNR's Radio Department, began to plan a series of scripts called "The Romance of Canada." The series would dramatize some major events in Canadian history. Author Merrill Denison was hired to write the scripts, and for twenty continuous weeks, he churned out episodes, often with large casts and complicated effects. Actor and director Tyrone Guthrie recalls the effort:

> We had good fun there. My colleagues were all railway workers, rather surprised to find themselves drafted into this newfangled nonsense of radio, and very much surprised to be mixed up with play-acting . . . . But gradually the pace began to tell. Halfway through the series, with about ten more scripts to write, poor Merrill was in trouble. He would deliver the current script just in time for the first rehearsal and then, exhausted, with no ideas, no enthusiasm, he would have to sit right down and beat his brains afresh. Furthermore, after the first ten or twelve installments he had used up the most familiar, as well as the most obviously "radiogenic" episodes in Canada's rather brief history.

Radio did create a new form of communication within Canada, but it also opened up the country to a whole new range of American influences. Radio had expanded far more rapidly in the United States than it had in Canada. The American stations were more numerous and more powerful, and their programming was slicker, more expensive and more varied. As a result some Canadian stations affiliated themselves with the big American networks in order to broadcast these shows. By 1930 most of the programs Canadians listened to were American ones, whether they were broadcast directly into Canada by U.S. stations or picked up by Canadian affiliates.

In 1928 a controversy over radio licences granted to the Jehovah's Witnesses led to an extensive debate in Parliament about Canadian broadcasting policy. J.S. Woodsworth argued strongly for public ownership as a defence against the Americanization of Canadian radio. The government responded by appointing a Royal Commission on Radio Broadcasting, headed by Sir John Aird, the president of the Bank of Commerce. In its 1929 report, the commission urged the government to bring private broadcasting under strict public regulation and to establish a publicly owned and financed broadcasting system. The coming of the Depression and the fall of the Liberal government in 1930 delayed any immediate action on the commission's report. Three years later in 1932, the Conservative government of R.B. Bennett implemented the commission's recommendations in a modified form with the creation of the Canadian Radio Broadcasting Commission (CRBC), the forerunner of the Canadian Broadcasting Corporation (CBC).

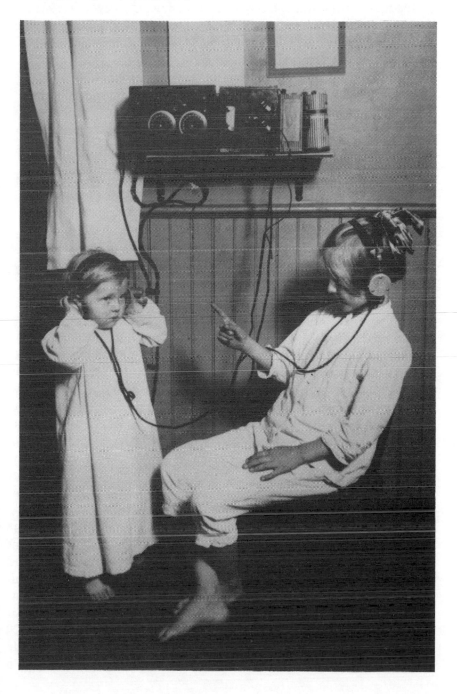

Listening to the radio in the early twenties. The most basic receiver was a crystal set, in which a wire "whisker" picked up radio signals from a piece of crystalline rock and transmitted them through earphones. Radio technology developed rapidly, however, and by the middle of the decade, more powerful equipment, with speakers instead of earphones, was available.

Hockey Salaries
The average salary for a hockey player in the NHL during the 1920s was $900.

Canada's success at the 1928 Olympic Games in Amsterdam was due to an outstanding track and field team. Percy Williams won two gold medals for the 100 and 200 metre sprints. James Ball won a silver in the 400 metre race, and the relay team, of which he was a member, won a bronze for the 1600 metre race.

The 1928 Games were the first in which women were allowed to compete, and Canada's women were just as successful as its men. Ethel Catherwood—the "Saskatoon Lily"—cleared 1.59 metres in the high jump to win a gold medal. Bobbie Rosenfeld won a silver medal in the 100 metre dash. She was also the lead runner on the women's relay team, which won a gold medal.

Sports

The broadcasting of professional sports soon became a great attraction on the radio. Foster Hewitt, a Toronto broadcaster, is best known as the original voice of "Hockey Night in Canada." In 1923, using an upright telephone, he did the first broadcast in history of a hockey game. His earliest broadcasts also included baseball commentaries which he made—accompanied by a few pigeons—from his perch atop Maple Leaf Stadium. His hockey broadcasts from Maple Leaf Gardens in Toronto began in 1931.

The American influence made itself felt in Canada in the world of professional sports too. Baseball at every level was popular. Most communities had amateur teams, and some had minor league professional teams. There was tremendous excitement when the Toronto Maple Leafs of the International League won the Little World Series in 1926. But it was major league baseball—America's national sport—that really captured Canadians' attention. Babe Ruth was just as much a hero in Canada as he was in the United States.

Baseball's chief rival for fans was Canada's own national sport, hockey. Between 1921 and 1924 three professional hockey leagues—two from the west, the Pacific Coast Hockey Association and the Western Canada Hockey League, and one from central Canada, the National Hockey League—battled it out for the Stanley Cup. In 1924 the two western leagues joined up to form the Western Hockey League, and the contest for the Stanley Cup became an east-west struggle.

There was another important development in 1924. Boston became the first American city to boast an NHL team. Hockey was becoming a North American rather than a strictly Canadian sport. The Boston Bruins were soon joined by teams in New York, Chicago and Detroit. The competition from big American money drove top-level professional hockey out of business in the west, and by 1927 six of the ten teams in the surviving league, the NHL, were American. In 1928 an American team, the New York Rangers, won the Stanley Cup for the first time.

By the late 1920s hockey had certainly become a North American game. Yet it was still very much Canadian in that almost all the players in the NHL were Canadians. A victory at the 1928 Olympics further underlined Canada's dominance in hockey. There were other athletic achievements in the 1920s that bolstered and unified Canadian national spirit. The Edmonton Grads, a women's basketball team, won frequent world championships in the 1920s in a sport a former Canadian, James Naismith, had invented. National championships were established in a number of sports, Canadian athletes made their best showing ever in Olympic competition at the 1928 games, and the Nova Scotia schooner *Bluenose* set an impressive winning record at sea.

1923

Movies

The drift towards a continental, U.S. dominated culture was most pronounced in the movie industry. Going to the movies became an enormously popular leisure activity in the 1920s. It was relatively inexpensive. Children could attend for less than ten cents, and adults usually paid somewhere between twenty-five and thirty-five cents. And movies were widely available. They were shown in meeting halls, schools and church basements; they were even incorporated into more traditional cultural events, such as the Wetaskiwin Fair where the townspeople might round off a day at the fairgrounds by going to the movies.

By the end of the decade, there were over 1000 movie houses and they were selling two million tickets a week. Almost all the movies these Canadian audiences were seeing came from Hollywood. In the early twenties, Canada had some success producing feature films. The most successful of these was *Back to God's Country* (1919), produced and directed by Ernest G. Shipman. By 1930, however, the American industry dominated cinema not just in Canada but around the world. Canada continued to produce talented performers, directors, writers and technical person-

The Edmonton Grads in 1923. Officially known as the Edmonton Commercial Graduates Basketball Club, the Grads were possibly the most successful team in Canadian sports history. They won 502 out of a total of 522 games they played. By the time the team broke up in 1940, it had won four Olympic medals.

Mary Pickford—
America's Sweetheart—
was born Gladys Mary
Smith in Toronto in 1893.
She began acting at the
age of five and by 1907
she was on Broadway.
Two years later she
began her film career
under the director D.W.
Griffith and became one
of the leading movie
stars of the day. With
her husband, Douglas
Fairbanks (left), and
Charlie Chaplin, she
founded United Artists
in 1919. In the 1920s she
starred in *Pollyanna*
(1920), *Little Lord
Fauntleroy* (1921), *Little
Annie Rooney* (1925) and
Coquette (1929), for
which she won an
Academy Award.

nel. Some of the biggest stars of the period, such as Mary Pickford, Norma Shearer and Marie Dressler, were Canadians. But
the film industry in Canada lacked the economic base to keep
that talent at home to compete with Hollywood.

In an attempt to keep some kind of film industry alive in
Canada, the governments of British Columbia and Ontario and
the federal government did create agencies to produce films but
the results, such as *Niagara the Glorious* and *Fishing Just for
Fun,* were decidedly inferior. It was not until 1939 when the federal agency, the Canadian Government Motion Picture Bureau,
was redeveloped as the National Film Board that a new attempt
was made to encourage a Canadian film industry. Canadian
culture in the 1920s seemed to be divided between contradictory
impulses towards nationalism on the one hand and Americanization on the other. When it came to the movies, the dominance of
the United States was unquestionable.

REVIEW AND DISCUSSION

Key People and Ideas
Explain the importance of each of the following as they are discussed in the chapter.

Tom Thomson	The Group of Seven
Emily Carr	*Canadian Forum*
Robert Stead	*Black Mask*
Morley Callaghan	*Mutt and Jeff*
E.J. Pratt	The Edmonton Grads
Foster Hewitt	Chautauqua
Mary Pickford	The Aird Commission

Analysing the Issues
Answer each of the following questions, which deal with important issues raised in the chapter.

1. Why was the Group of Seven successful?
2. What role did sport have in Canadian cultural life in the twenties?
3. What were the effects of prohibition?
4. What impact did radio have on Canadian culture in the 1920s?

Questions for Discussion
Think carefully about each of the following questions and discuss the issues which they raise.

1. Canadian culture in the 1920s was open to many influences from the United States. Explain which you think was the dominant cultural trend, nationalism or continentalism. Is the same true today?
2. Culture can include everything from poetry and painting to hockey and country fairs. Are some kinds of cultural activities more important than others? Be prepared to defend your case, using examples from the twenties.

EPILOGUE

By the end of the decade, Elsie Freeman had spent ten years as a seamstress, moving from company to company within the textile trade. In 1929 she was working for two dressmaking partners, Scott and Livingstone. The stock market collapse in October of that year broke up the partnership and, for a time, Elsie Freeman found herself unemployed. But not for long. Both Scott and Livingstone relocated in separate, competing dress factories and began to rehire their old employees. To attract Elsie Freeman, Scott offered her higher wages than Livingstone. In this climate of ill will and worker insecurity, Elsie Freeman returned to Scott —with a higher wage than her co-workers. Once the secret was out, she was ostracized by her fellow workers for earning more than they did.

Elsie was able to put money aside for a trip to England. She was not married and had few financial responsibilities other than her room and board, which amounted to $5.00 a week and included three meals a day. In 1930 she earned $16.50 for a forty-four-hour work week including a half-day on Saturday. Little competition from foreign-made clothing meant that seamstresses were in constant demand, since Canadians had to dress themselves no matter how tough times became.

As Elsie was preparing for her trip abroad, the Blind Institute offered her a job making difficult pieces of dresses which blind women would then finish using their superb sense of touch. Unfortunately, the blind seamstresses became suspicious of Elsie, once they realized she could see. They thought she was a threat to their employment.

Elsie Freeman in the mid-twenties with "bobbed" hair. Short haircuts, which many older people thought were unfeminine and improper, were just one of the new styles which young women like Elsie adopted in the twenties. The new freedom in dress and appearance went along with the new opportunities women were seeking in education, politics and employment.

No matter what I said, the blind girls were convinced that I was taking their work. You've no idea how uncomfortable that made me feel. I left the job as soon as my savings were large enough for the trip to England.

I sailed for England on the *RMS Laurentic*, a steamship which belonged to the White Star Line. Ever since coming to Toronto in 1920, I had been admiring the beautiful advertisements in the newspapers that promised luxury and excitement aboard those gigantic passenger liners. Initially it seemed that only the rich could afford to travel but, by the end of the twenties, lots of people were travelling back and forth to Europe. We ate like royalty and partied all the way across the Atlantic, with dances and games filling each day and night. If ten years working as a seamstress were needed to pay for this trip, I would have to say it was worth it.

Unfortunately, when I got back, the Depression was in full swing. Wages were the same but my landlady raised her room and board to $6.00 a week—because she thought I was rich, I guess. Seamstresses were still in demand, and I got a variety of jobs in the thirties making dresses and underwear. But I had to cut back on my entertainment considerably, as did all my friends. We ceased to think of world travel and concentrated on more local entertainment. Amusement parks became popular. Sunnyside Beach was the biggest, with roller coaster rides, miniature golf courses and dance halls. For summer excursions, large lake steamers ferried weekend crowds back and forth from Toronto to Port Dalhousie and Niagara several times a day.

I suppose the shock of the Depression had a settling effect on my generation. I was soon married and raising a family, much to the relief of my parents who thought the carefree climate of the twenties was destroying my values. When I think of those years it is always with fondness. I was young, and it seemed the whole country was changing before my eyes, and I wanted to become part of the new industrial society in which women bobbed their hair and wore freer clothing. Politics didn't interest me as much as the ferment of city life. Automobiles, dances, sports and travel were part of the spirit of the twenties. But pride in becoming a skilled worker and finding a place in the work force was the most important thing in my life, as it was with most of my girlfriends.

For Elsie Freeman, even the shock of the Depression could not shake the independence she had achieved through those ten years that changed so much in Canadian life. Her experiences captured much of the spirit of the decade.

Elsie wasn't one of those who "made it big" in the city, but her life during the twenties was probably more exciting and less difficult than that of most Canadians. The contrast would become even greater during the "dirty thirties." From the depths of the Depression, the twenties would look like good times even to the many who never made it at all.

Further Reading

- Allen, Richard. *The Social Passion: Religion and Social Reform in Canada, 1914-1928.* Toronto: University of Toronto Press, 1970. Explores all aspects of progressivism and the social gospel.
- Bennett, Paul W. and Jaenen, Cornelius J. *Emerging Identities: Selected Problems and Interpretations in Canadian History.* Toronto: Prentice-Hall, 1986. Includes accounts of Maritime protest movements and the women's movement in the 1920s.
- Berger, Carl and Cook, Ramsay. *The West and the Nation.* Toronto: McClelland and Stewart, 1976. Analyzes the development of the west's political influence in the 1920s.
- Bondy, Robert J. and Mattys, William C. *The Confident Years: Canada in the 1920s.* Toronto: Prentice-Hall, 1978. A social history of the twenties in scrapbook form, with cartoons, photographs, ads, excerpts from newspapers, books, catalogues, government reports.
- *Canada's Illustrated Heritage: The Crazy Twenties 1920/1930.* Toronto: McClelland and Stewart, 1978. A lively, readable and well-illustrated social history of the twenties.
- Dawson, Robert MacGregor and Neatby, H. Blair. *William Lyon Mackenzie King.* 3 vols. Toronto: University of Toronto Press, 1976. The official biography of King provides a thorough analysis of the political challenges, policies and problems of the King years.
- Graham, William. *Arthur Meighen: A Biography.* 3 vols. Toronto: Clarke, Irwin, 1965. Arthur Meighen has not been as well documented as his arch rival, King, but this biography offers insight into this forceful man who failed to find his moment in history.
- Granatstein, J.L., Abella, Irving M., Bercuson, David J., Brown, R. Craig, Neatby, H. Blair. *Twentieth Century Canada.* Toronto: McGraw-Hill Ryerson Limited, 1986. An outstanding survey of modern Canadian history by some of the best current historians.
- Kealey, Gregory S. and Warrian, Peter, eds. *Essays in Canadian Working Class History.* Toronto: McClelland and Stewart, 1976. Includes an essay by David Frank on class conflict in the coal industry in Cape Breton.
- MacInnis, Grace. *J.S. Woodsworth: A Man to Remember.* Toronto: Macmillan, 1953. Grace MacInnis, the daughter of J.S. Woodsworth, provides a scholarly yet personal view of her father.
- McNaught, Kenneth. *A Prophet in Politics: A Biography of J.S. Woodsworth.* Toronto: University of Toronto Press, 1959. An outstanding and sensitive study of an important political figure.
- Morton, W.L. *The Progressive Party in Canada.* Toronto: University of Toronto Press, 1967. An excellent examination of the role of farm protest movements in Canadian political life in the 1920s.
- Oliver, Peter N. *G. Howard Ferguson: Ontario Tory.* Toronto: University of Toronto Press, 1977. An able study of Ontario Premier Howard Ferguson and provincial politics in the 1920s.
- Stacey, C.P. *A Very Double Life: The Private World of Mackenzie King.* Toronto: Macmillan, 1976. A fascinating biography which focuses on the private eccentricities of the prime minister.
- Stead, Robert J.C. *Grain.* Toronto: McClelland and Stewart, 1963; *The Homesteaders.* Toronto: University of Toronto Press, 1973. Reprints of two of Robert Stead's novels, which were popular in the 1920s.
- Thompson, John Herd, with Seager, Allen. *Canada: 1922-1939: Decades of Discord.* Toronto: McClelland and Stewart, 1985. A detailed account of Canadian history in the 1920s and 1930s.

Index

Page numbers in italics refer to illustrations, captions and/or margin notes.